A PRACTICAL GUIDE TO AUTOCAD AUTOLISP

A Practical Guide to
AutoCAD AutoLISP

Trevor Bousfield

LONGMAN

Addison Wesley Longman Limited
Edinburgh Gate, Harlow
Essex CM20 2JE, England
and Associated Companies throughout the world

© Addison Wesley Longman Limited 1998

First published 1998

British Library Cataloguing in Publication Data
A catalogue entry for this title is available from the British Library

ISBN 0-582-32673-7

Set by 35 in 10/13pt Times
Produced by Addison Wesley Longman Singapore (Pte) Ltd
Printed in Singapore

Contents

Preface

This book was written for a wide audience, in fact all the many thousands of AutoCAD users worldwide. Students in colleges and universities and experienced AutoCAD users can benefit from customisation in order to solve their specific problems.

There is no doubt whatsoever of the rewards which will be experienced and gained from a small input which will confirm to the reader the true value of the high-level language AutoLISP.

Students using AutoCAD will find this book invaluable, and in particular the section relating to the study of the City & Guilds schemes, the BTEC and SCOTVEC National and Higher National schemes, as well as under-graduates and post-graduates at higher education institutes and universities.

The users of AutoCAD employed on a commercial basis will find this book a constant source of reference.

Learning will take place by a series of worked examples all based on realistic practical tutorials selected from recent experience, and having meaningful value to the user in providing solutions to a specific problem.

The book presumes that the reader will have access to a computer which is capable of running AutoCAD Release 12 or 13 under Windows or DOS, and have at least a basic knowledge of running the software for draughting purposes. The book presents a natural progression through the City & Guilds 4351 scheme, from the basic *Computer aided draughting and design* (4351–001) through *Three-dimensional design* (4351–003) and *Customisation and system management* (4351–004), to *AutoLISP Programming* (4351–005).

AutoLISP programs have been input either in the DOS version from the text editor, or by using word processing software in 'non-document' mode. Most word processors have this facility.

The programs illustrated are available for download on the Internet; however, to fully understand the routines and create your own AutoLISP programs the creation and inputing from keyboard will need to be practised.

The book has been written in three parts to cater for the varying needs of the reader.

Part One *AutoLISP in Action* is written for the reader with little or no knowledge of AutoLISP. This section consists of exercises designed to demonstrate a series of basic rules necessary for the beginner in AutoLISP.

Part Two *Advanced AutoLISP* can be the starting point for the more experienced AutoLISP user. Most of the exercises are graphical problems, as these tend to be more applicable to specific industrial problems and ideal for customisation.

Both these parts have graded exercises at the end of each learning experience to help test the reader's knowledge.

Part Three *City & Guilds AutoLISP Programming* is designed for the student who wishes to qualify for a City & Guilds *AutoLISP Programming* Certificate (C&G 4351–005). The text is written for external candidates as well as those studying on a recognised AutoCAD course within an institute.

I wish to acknowledge the help that Neville Cumberland has given me in editing the text and preparing the illustrations, and would also like to acknowledge the considerable contribution made to the final editing by Brett Gilbert; not forgetting the continued support, over the years, of Joan, Ian and Howard.

Trevor Bousfield
June 1997

Internet

The programs and macros included in this book are available on the Addison Wesley Longman website, at the following address:

ftp://ftp.awl.co.uk/pub/awl-he/engineering/bousfield

Information about this book and related titles can be found at the Longman Higher Education website:

http://awl-he.co.uk

Introduction – Why AutoLISP?

The question is like asking 'Why AutoCAD?' since both AutoLISP and AutoCAD are synonymous with successful solutions to design problems for more years than many wish to admit.

Visit those businesses who have responded to the challenge of AutoLISP as a tool for customising their particular problems to see the benefit of automated systems within the production of computer graphics.

The latest release of AutoCAD (Release 14) has benefited from such developments by incorporating a system of layer settings achieved by simply selecting objects visible on the screen. It is now over seven years since I published the very same solution by using an AutoLISP macro.

What are we to do as designers, if we recognise the limitations of AutoCAD to solve a particular problem?

You could try to buy your way out of the problem. This, however, can be time consuming and expensive.

Or you could do nothing.

I prefer to solve the problem by writing an AutoLISP macro. I have used this experience to encourage other designers to do likewise. Between 1989 and 1992 I published a series of articles in CADuser Magazine on AutoLISP, designed specifically to encourage AutoCAD users to solve their own particular problems.

This book is simply an extension of that process.

'Why AutoLISP? – Why not?'

Note about program presentation

The continuation of the lines of a program that are too long to fit on a single line with the book is shown using a curved arrow. When typing these lines replace the arrow with a space and continue the text below on the same line.

For instance, take the program presented below:

```
INTRO.LSP
(DEFUN C:INTRO ()
 (GRAPHSCR)
 (SETQ STR1 (GETSTRING ⏎
        "PLEASE ENTER YOUR NAME: "))
 (SETQ STR2 " to AutoLISP") (TERPRI)
 (PRINC "Welcome ")⏎
        (PRINC STR1) (PRINC STR2)
 (PRINC)
)
```

When entering this program at the keyboard, you should type it as follows:

```
INTRO.LSP
(DEFUN C:INTRO ()
 (GRAPHSCR)
 (SETQ STR1 (GETSTRING "PLEASE ENTER YOUR NAME: "))
 (SETQ STR2 " to AutoLISP") (TERPRI)
 (PRINC "Welcome ") (PRINC STR1) (PRINC STR2)
 (PRINC)
)
```

Part One
AutoLISP in Action

Introduction

There are three different programming languages that communicate with AutoCAD:

- AutoLISP
- ADS
- ARX

AutoLISP was, in 1986, the first programming language to be offered. By October 1990 a C programming language was introduced called ADS (Autodesk Development System). This system communicates via AutoLISP, but because ADS applications are compiled, they run faster than AutoLISP. However, the fact that AutoLISP is not compiled means that it can be entered directly at the AutoCAD command prompt.

In 1995, ARX (AutoCAD Runtime Extension) was introduced with Release 13 as a replacement for ADS as a response to ever-increasing demands on speed. This is achieved by bypassing the AutoLISP interpreter and communicating directly with the AutoCAD code.

AutoLISP is the easiest of the three languages to learn.

> *AutoLISP is based on the LISP programming language, which is simple to learn yet very powerful.*

AutoCAD Manual

It is worth stating that most people operating a CAD station, such as designers, have no desire to become a computer programmer. So the question is: Why learn AutoLISP?

To answer this, have a closer look at AutoCAD. The intention has always been to recognise the need for user customisation of the software. In the early days of AutoCAD this policy led to some sacrifice in terms of speed, which was quickly pounced upon by envious competitors (envious of AutoCADs' share of the market).

This policy was a clear recognition of the expertise in terms of customisation needs being firmly held by those practising the technology, hence the need for a high-level language to be readily accessible by those people operating CAD systems such as designers. The solution to your particular problem may be within your own hands in the form of AutoLISP ... It is designed to be used by those of us who make no claims to be expert programmers, but who wish to solve everyday problems without a heavy investment in time.

AutoLISP in Action:
A series of 30 articles published in the
CADuser Magazine by Trevor Bousfield (1989)

Using AutoLISP in direct mode

You can use AutoLISP as a simple calulator (in 'direct mode'). For instance, at the command prompt enter the following:

```
(*  3  16)   i.e. multiply three by sixteen; note the result
(+  3  16)   i.e. add three and sixteen; note the result
(-  16  3)   i.e. subtract three from sixteen; note the result
(/  3  16)   i.e. divide three by sixteen; note the result
```

Rule 1
The first entity following a left-hand parenthesis must be a function followed by space.

You have just performed a number of functions, i.e. multiplication, addition, subtraction, etc.

One of the first things you notice about AutoLISP is all the parentheses. In fact some would say that the acronym 'LISP' stands for 'Lots of Incredibly Stupid Parentheses'!

Rule 2
Every opening parenthesis must have a corresponding closing parenthesis, otherwise AutoLISP will display an error message.

As you build up or add parenthesis, you 'nest' the functions inside each other as you will soon see, however, the problem is no greater than the need to count each left hand parenthesis and each right hand parenthesis to make sure that they balance.

At the command prompt enter the following:

```
(+ (/ 10 2) 6)
```

The AutoLISP evaluator operates on the inner-most bracket first: dividing 10 by 2 and then adding 6. This should display the value 11.

At the command prompt enter the whole of the following line:

```
(PROMPT "THIS IS FUN"); and note the result
```

AutoLISP ignores everything to the right-hand side of the semicolon (the ';') which acts in the same way as the REM ('remark') command in the BASIC programming language.

■ **Question**: What then is the benefit of including '; and note the result'?

You have just used the AutoLISP function PROMPT, there are many more to learn.

■ **Question**: Do we need to learn them or can we simply rely on the AutoLISP manual?

Let's return to our simple sums. At the command prompt enter:

```
(* PI 35)
```

The number PI already has a value in AutoLISP (22/7). The resultant output is therefore the circumference of a circle with a diameter of 35 units. It is possible to set a value for a variable 'D' (diameter) by using a function called SETQ. At the command prompt enter:

```
(SETQ D 35)
```

In plain English, 'let D equal 35'. This value is now stored in the computer memory, test this by entering '!D' and noting the result. If we now return to our original calculation for the circumference of a circle:

```
(* PI D)
```

Note the result.

Why don't we attach the answer to a variable such as 'C' for circumference? In this way the answer will be held in the computer's memory as long as we remain in the drawing editor or until we replace this value with a new value.

```
(SETQ C (* PI D))
```

Note the balanced parentheses. Now enter '!C', again noting the result.

These variables can also be used as values within the standard AutoCAD commands. At the command prompt enter:

```
(SETQ TEST 4.123)
```

Now enter the following:

```
CIRCLE
3P/2P/TTR/<CENTRE POINT>:  Type a value or pick a point
DIAMETER/<RADIUS>:  Type !TEST
```

Note the result. These variables lose their values when you exit the current drawing.

Lets return once more to our simple sums. Enter:

```
(/ 7 2)
```

Note the result. The wrong answer is given because AutoLISP has divided one *integer* by another *integer*, and returned the answer as an *integer*.

To avoid this problem try:

```
(/ 7.0 2)
```

This time we used a *real* number '7.0' in the calculation resulting in a *real* answer. Also try:

```
(/ 5 .5)
```

Note the result.

Rule 3

Always enter one of the values as a real number by adding a decimal point, to avoid errors in calculations.

There are many more maths functions available for you to use at a later date.

Creating AutoLISP programs

AutoLISP programs need to be created in 'non-document' mode, sometimes referred to as ASCII text. Most leading word processors have this feature, but many people will have one of the much simpler text-editing programs such as EDLIN, and for small AutoLISP programs I have yet to be convinced that there is any need to use a 'proper' word processor. I have used EDLIN and my instructions assume that you will be too. If not you may find that your editor operates slightly differently from EDLIN.

Defining a function

You can think of AutoCAD commands such as LINE, CIRCLE, ARC, etc. as functions. There is no reason why you can't create your own functions to automate the tasks that you need to perform repeatedly.

User-defined functions (small programs, often called 'macro's) contain many instructions and it would be impractical to spread them out in one long horizontal line, bounded by parentheses. It is much more practical to format the program in a vertical structure containing lines of functions or instructions with an opening parenthesis at the start of the first line and a closing parenthesis on the final line of the AutoLISP program.

```
( . . . . . . . . .
  . . . . . . . . .
  . . . . . . . . .
)
```

Once this program is saved, it can be loaded for use at any time. You can give it an AutoCAD command name of your choice.

Now for our first user-defined function. Access the EDLIN program from the DOS prompt, or type 'EDIT' from within AutoCAD. (The AutoCAD ACAD.PGP file would need to be amended appropriately to allow this 'EDIT' command to work.)

Now enter the following:

```
INTRO.LSP
(DEFUN C:INTRO ()
```

```
(GRAPHSCR)
(SETQ STR1 (GETSTRING "PLEASE ENTER YOUR NAME: "))
(SETQ STR2 " to AutoLISP") (TERPRI)
(PRINC "Welcome ") (PRINC STR1) (PRINC STR2)
(PRINC)
)
```

Save the program by entering 'E' for 'end'. You can now load the macro into the drawing editor; at the command prompt enter:

```
(LOAD "INTRO")
```

Now check that the macro has been successfully loaded by entering:

```
INTRO
```

Congratulations! You have just completed your first AutoLISP program, however, we need some explanation and we need to establish good practice.

■ **Question**: What would happen if you try to use a space when you enter your name in INTRO.LSP?

Rule 4

You should resist the temptation to simplify your program (as I have done above) by omitting any informative notes. Always add helpful comments to your programs (by using a semicolon) to remind yourself (and others) what the program does.

Let's go through the functions you have used in INTRO.LSP:

■ **GRAPHSCR** – This causes the screen to flip from text mode to graphics mode when only one screen is in use (AutoCAD is written for two screens); it is similar to pressing the 'F1' key (or 'F2' in AutoCAD Release 13 (or higher) for Windows).

■ **GETSTRING** – One of a family of functions (similar to GET in BASIC) that waits for an input from the user, in this case a alphanumeric text 'string', it should always be associated with some form of screen prompt.

■ **TERPRI** – Starts the next prompt on a new line.

■ **PRINC** – Prints the string on the screen or, in the case of a variable such as 'STR1', prints the value of the variable. The final PRINC in the program is often referred to as a 'clean exit'.

Rule 5

Always re-load an AutoLISP program after every modification or editing session. This will replace the last version in memory and force AutoCAD to use the updated program.

We will now apply our newly acquired programming skills to the solution of simple graphical problems.

The first graphical program will construct a rectangle to our requirements. Using EDLIN enter the following program:

```
REC.LSP
(DEFUN C:REC ()
 (GRAPHSCR)
 (SETQ P1 (GETPOINT "PICK THE BOTTOM L.H. CORNER"))⏎
      (TERPRI)
 (SETQ P3 (GETCORNER P1 "PICK THE TOP R.H. CORNER"))⏎
      (TERPRI)
 (SETQ P2 (LIST (CAR P3) (CADR P1)))
 (SETQ P4 (LIST (CAR P1) (CADR P3)))
 (COMMAND "PLINE" P1 P2 P3 P4 "C")
)
```

The above program helps to illustrate one of the major advantages of the AutoLISP language for programming graphics (see Figure 1).

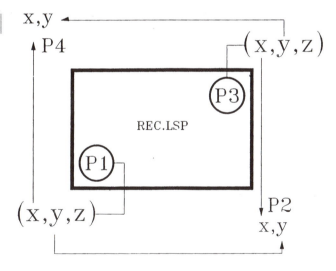

Figure 1

As engineers and designers with a strong tradition in the basic rules of algebra, we have no problem in accepting one value for one variable (for example 'P1' = 36) or, in terms of a single point in space, we could state 'P1' is a combination of 'x' = 20, 'y' = 46 and 'z' = 24.5, i.e. one value (in this case a single point in space) for one variable. The advantage of AutoLISP is just this: that a *list* of values can be associated with one variable.

Notice 'P1' and 'P3' in the REC.LSP program. These variables both represent points in space and contain values for 'x', 'y' and 'z' (coordinates of a point). However, you can't generate such a list simply as '(20 46 24.5)' because, as you will notice, we have broken Rule 1. There must always be a function after the opening parenthesis (except when using an apostrophe) followed by a space. Hence the correct syntax is '(LIST 20 46 24.5)' – no points for guessing the name of *that* function! There are no limits to the type or length of a LIST.

Rule 6
If in doubt leave a space! (But not in the case of menus.)

There are many ways of extracting values from listed variables such as 'P1' and 'P2' above. CAR and CADR are the most commonly used functions for extracting information from a LIST:

■ **CAR** – Returns the first item of the list.
■ **CADR** – Extracts the second item from a list.

There are other similar functions.
But for the moment concentrate on P2 and P4 above (see Figure 1):

'P2' = 'x' value of 'P3' and the 'y' value of 'P1'
'P4' = 'x' value of 'P1' and the 'y' value of 'P3'

AutoCAD commands

AutoLISP lets you access most AutoCAD commands from within the program, thus enabling you to create graphics with an AutoLISP macro.

Rule 7
The names of the AutoCAD commands and sub-commands are always enclosed in quotation marks, with empty quotation marks used to represent pressing the 'Enter' key. (**Hint**: If you are not sure of the sequence of sub-commands test the function out in direct mode before completing the AutoLISP macro.)

You may wish to add comments to the REC.LSP program prior to loading and running. When loading the program you should see 'C:REC' in the prompt area of the screen. The 'C' has nothing to do with your hard disk drive. It means that AutoCAD now recognises 'REC' as a new AutoCAD command.

Setting out your program

It is good practice to indent the AutoLISP program:

```
(DEFUN etc.
  (GRAPHSCR)
   (SETQ etc.
    (WHILE etc.
      (COMMAND etc.)
    )
   )
 )
```

Rule 8

When the closing parenthesis for a function is not on the same horizontal line as the opening parenthesis, make sure that it is in line vertically, and that no other entries occupy the vertical space between the two parentheses (see the last line of REC.LSP).

A practical problem

Now for something more ambitious (and practical).

The content of the published articles in the CADuser Magazine were in the main solutions to readers' problems, some from as far afield as Europe. However, one of the first problems to be solved came from an engineering company in York. The problem involved repetitive shapes, representing insulation between two walls. The standard shape had to be repeated over variable lengths at any possible angle.

The solution involves a series of AutoCAD commands such as:

```
(COMMAND "PLINE" P1 P2 ...)
```

It is possible to include AutoLISP functions within the AutoCAD function such as:

```
(COMMAND "PLINE" (SETQ P1(LIST 100 100))
            (SETQ P2 (LIST 200 200)) ...)
```

I don't find much point in the above method but it is for you to select the most appropriate solution for your needs.

The program INS.LSP (below) shows the solution (see Figure 2): 'P1' and 'P2' are the selected end points with the shape being created at point 'P1' prior to being rotated in the direction of 'P2'. The ARRAY command is then used to repeat the shape between points 'P1' and 'P2', however, the X axis of the user coordinate system has to be rotated in the direction of 'P2' prior to the use of the ARRAY command.

Figure 2

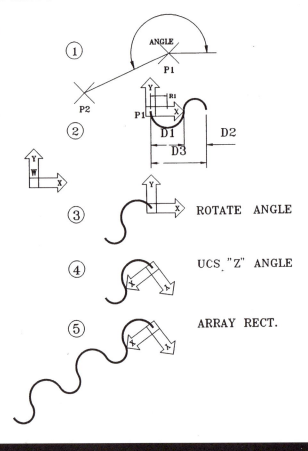

ROTATE   ANGLE

UCS "Z" ANGLE

ARRAY RECT.

INS.LSP

```
(DEFUN C:INS ()
 (GRAPHSCR)
  (SETQ P1 (GETPOINT "PLEASE SELECT THE START POINT "))(TERPRI)
  (COMMAND "UCS" "O" P1)
  (SETQ P1 (LIST 0 0))
  (SETQ P2 (GETPOINT "PLEASE SELECT THE END POINT "))(TERPRI)
  (SETQ D (DISTANCE P1 P2))
  (SETQ N (/ D 10)) ; 10= NOMINAL LENGTH OF SHAPE
  (SETQ NI (FIX N)) ; CREATE INTEGER
  (SETQ LE (/ D NI)) ; ACTUAL LENGTH OF SHAPE
  (SETQ Q (ANGLE P1 P2))
  (SETQ Q1 (* Q (/ 180 PI))) ; ANGLE IN DEGREES
  (SETQ D1 (* 0.6 LE) D2 (* 0.4 LE) R1 (/ D1 2) D3 (+ D1 D2))
  (COMMAND "PLINE" P1 "A" "CE" (LIST R1 0) (LIST D1 0) (LIST D3 0)"")
   (COMMAND "ROTATE" "L" "" P1 Q1)
   (COMMAND "UCS" "Z" Q1)
   (COMMAND "ARRAY" "L" "" "R" 1 NI LE)
   (COMMAND "UCS" "P")
   (COMMAND "UCS" "P")
)
```

■ **DISTANCE** – This calculates the distance between two points, 'P1' and 'P2', via the GETPOINT function of a LIST of coordinate values.

■ **FIX** – Truncates a fractional quantity (a *real* number) resulting in an *integer*. In the use of our example, we wish to know how many complete shapes will fit between points 'P1' and 'P2'.

■ **ANGLE** – Calculate the angle formed by an imaginary line drawn between points 'P1' and 'P2'. Using a horizontal reference line (at the three o'clock position) in an anti-clockwise direction, measured in radians.

As a former engineer and designer, the use of degrees for the measurement of angles was a natural first choice, with radians relegated to memories of former academic activities.

AutoCAD commands use degrees to denote angles whilst AutoLISP uses radians. There is, therefore, the need to convert the value of an angle in degrees to its value in radians, and vice versa.

If like me your natural instinct is to use degrees, then I urge you to abandon such thoughts when you begin to design your AutoLISP macros involving graphical angles.

Rule 9
Think radians at all times when using AutoLISP functions.

Load INS.LSP and run the program, selecting points 'P1' and 'P2' at various lengths and angles to test the program. Because the length of each shape is calculated to be as near as possible to 10 units it is assumed that the distance between 'P1' and 'P2' is at least 10 units in length.

Looping the loop

The example given in INS.LSP involved repeated shapes and could also have been solved by the use of the MINSERT command.

Loops allow programs to be repeated automatically until a test condition is satisfied (a little bit like the ARRAY command in INS.LSP). An AutoCAD loop you will already be familiar with is the LINE command with the test condition being an empty 'Enter' key (this breaks you out of the loop). Loops are a great help when solving problems with AutoLISP.

In AutoLISP there are three different loop functions available. My preferred function is REPEAT. It is necessary when using this function to state the number of times the program or part of the program is to be repeated.

For our first example of loops, we will construct an arc, not because we wish to 'outdo' the ARC AutoCAD command but because this method forms the basis for the solution of more complex problems, such as producing involutes, spirals, cams, cone development, etc.

The solution is shown in MARC.LSP and in Figure 3.

MARC.LSP

```
(DEFUN C:MARC ()
 (GRAPHSCR)
  (SETQ P0 (GETPOINT "PLEASE PICK THE CENTRE OF ARC"))(TERPRI)
  (COMMAND "UCS" "O" P0)
  (SETQ P0 (LIST 0 0) R 100 P1 (LIST R 0) A (/ PI 180))
   (REPEAT 90
     (SETQ X (* R (COS A))
           Y (* R (SIN A))
           P2 (LIST X Y)
   )
     (COMMAND "LINE" P1 P2 "")
     (SETQ P1 P2)
     (SETQ A (+ A (/ PI 180)))
   )               ; END OF LOOP
   (COMMAND "UCS" "P")
 )                 ; END OF FUNCTION.
```

Figure 3

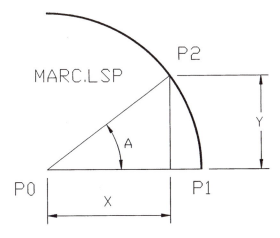

P2

MARC.LSP

A

P0   P1

X

ANGLE A EXAGGERATED FOR CLARITY

PI/180 (Radians) = 1 Degree

The function is based upon lines drawn between the points 'P1' and 'P2'. Each 'P2' becomes the new 'P1' each time angle 'A' is increased causing the ARC to be generated from a series of vectors (in this case 90 vectors).

Don't be concerned that the ARC is in fact a series of vectors, this is no different to the AutoCAD ARC or CIRCLE commands; the difference is simply the number of vectors used within a given angle, and therefore the accuracy of the curve.

- **MARC.LSP** – 'Modified ARC'; don't name the AutoLISP program ARC if you wish to use the ARC AutoCAD command.
- **REPEAT** – This is the start of the loop which calculates the points 'P1' and 'P2' before drawing a line between the two points, these lines are drawn 90 times in the loop before the program continues to the next line in the program. Angle 'A' = $\pi/180$ radians = 1 degree, hence the included angle of the completed arc = 90 degrees.

Note: It is not necessary to repeat functions when there are a number of similar functions in a program, such as SETQ and COMMAND. Notice program lines 5, 7, 8, 9 and 13. Grouping similar functions in this way can simplify programs.

More loops

In the above solution the number of repeats in the loop was known. If this is not the case then a test condition must be specified within the program to enable the loop to continue as long as a certain condition is true (or until the 'not true' condition is identified). This may appear complicated, but it is not.

For example, a test condition could be: 'Work as hard as you can until you are hungry.' Your stomach becomes the test condition.

To repeat an expression as long as the result is true:

```
(SETQ X 0)
  (WHILE (<= X 10)
  (SETQ X (+ 1 X)
)
```

Remember that zero is a valid value in computing; this loop will repeat as long as 'X' is equal to any value below 11.

```
(SETQ X 0)
  (WHILE X
   (SETQ etc
   (COMMAND etc
   (IF (TEST CONDITION) (SETQ X NIL))
)
```

This loop will repeat as long as 'X' has a value. When the test condition is satisfied, then 'X' is set to NIL and the program will proceed to the next line. This 'if then else' statement is the most popular function for controlling decisions. *If* the test condition is true *then* carry out the instruction *else* continue (if there is no alternative instruction).

Rule 10

Never use zero as a variable value if you really mean NIL; there is a difference. (Also take care with P1 ('one') and PI (capital 'I') – this is often the cause of failure.)

Let's put our new knowledge to the solution of a practical problem: The development of a cone from a parametric input – see CONE.LSP and Figure 4.

CONE.LSP

```
(DEFUN C:CONE ()
 (GRAPHSCR)
  (SETQ R (GETDIST "\nPLEASE ENTER THE CONE RADIUS: "))
  (SETQ H (GETDIST "\nPLEASE ENTER THE HEIGHT OF CONE: "))
  (SETQ P1 (GETPOINT "\nPLEASE PICK THE APEX OF CONE: "))
  (COMMAND "UCS" "O" P1)
  (SETQ P1 (LIST 0 0) P2 (LIST R (- H))
        P3 (LIST (- R) (- H)) D (DISTANCE P1 P2)
        P5 (POLAR P1 0 D)
  )
```
➡

```
(COMMAND "LINE" P5 P1 P2 P3 P1 "") ; DRAW THE CONE
(SETQ RA (/ (* 2 PI R) D) A 0.035 I "T")
  (WHILE I
    (SETQ P4 (POLAR P1 A D))
    (COMMAND "LINE" P5 P4 "")
    (SETQ P5 P4 A (+ A 0.035))
      (IF (> A RA)(SETQ I NIL)) ; TEST CONDITION FOR LOOP
  )                             ; END OF LOOP.
    (COMMAND "LINE" P4 P1 "")
    (PRINC)
)
```

Figure 4

(LENGTH OF ARC= PI*2*R (circumference of base of cone)

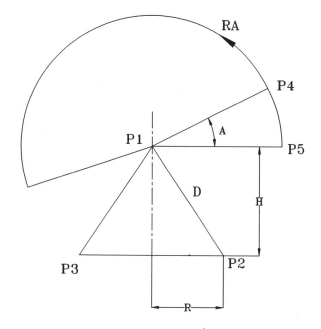

$$RADIANS = ARC/RAD$$

$$HENCE, \quad RA = 2*PI*R/D$$

ANGLE A EXAGGERATED FOR CLARITY
ANGLE A= PI/90 (Radians)= app. 0.035 (app 2 Degrees)

See, for example, CADuser Magazine, September 1988 – when this program was published a helpful typist entered '(SETQ I 0)' instead of my function '(SETQ I NIL)'.

The above error in the program caused an *endless* loop and the program ran continuously and could only be terminated with a 'Ctrl+C' keystroke, or in some cases, by switching off the computer.

> ### Rule 11
> Take special care when using loops to define an end in the loop.

Parameter brackets ()

So far I have given no explanation for the empty brackets at the end of the DEFUN function name.

These brackets can be used to declare the program variables as 'local' variables, such as:

```
(DEFUN C:CONE (/ R H P1 P2 P3 P4 P5 D RA A)
```

This would have the effect of returning the value of each variable to NIL after running the program.

> ### Rule 12
> Local variables must be listed following a forward slash.

Variables which are not declared as local are known as 'global' variables. Their values remain in memory until overwritten during the current drawing session.

> ### Rule 13
> Do not declare local variables until you have tested the program.

When debugging a program it is important to be able to check the value of certain variables at the command prompt. If a variable such as 'RA' retains a value of NIL in the above program, check to see if variables 'R' and 'D' have values; if this is the case, then the error is detected within the '(SETQ RA ...)' function.

Control characters

Notice the change to the GET functions. Instead of using TERPRI to force the prompt on to a new line. I have used one of the five available control codes. When you insert '\n' immediately before the prompt text the prompt statement is forced to a new line. There is no need to use a lower case 'n', but it helps with the reading to mix lower and upper case, as shown in CONE.LSP.

Polar function

Refer to the (SETQ P4 ...) function in CONE.LSP. Up to this point we have used cartesian coordinates (x, y, z) to define 'P1', 'P2', etc. A very useful function which often simplifies programming is the POLAR function.

This function is always available using ATTITUDE. Jog your memory by using the LINE command from a point and note the value in the status area of the screen as you move the mouse or puck (press F6). This value is a 'polar' coordinate showing the distance and angle from the start point of the line (the angle is given in degrees).

The AutoLISP POLAR function is the reverse of the ATTITUDE function, joining the angle in radians (anti-clockwise from the three-o'clock position) followed by the distance. Hence:

```
(SETQ P4 (POLAR P1 A D))
```

While loop

Notice that the variable 'I' was given a value prior to the loop (SETQ ... I "T") – I have used 'T' for 'true'. In this way the loop continues to repeat until 'I' = NIL.

For example, enter the following:

```
(WHILE (PRINC (GETPOINT"\nPICK A POINT: ")))
```

1. Pick a number of points note the effect of the PRINC function.
2. Now press 'Enter', noting the result when the WHILE function is no longer true.

Test functions

Notice the test condition used in CONE.LSP:

```
(IF (> A RA) ...)
```

AutoLISP provides a range of functions to test for certain conditions, returning either TRUE or NIL depending on whether the function meets the test condition. The function would be true if angle 'A' is greater than angle 'RA'.

There are many more test functions available but for the moment we will restrict our checking to number functions, such as:

```
<    less than
>    greater than
<=   less than or equal to
>=   greater than or equal to
/=   not equal to
=    equal (also EQ and EQUAL functions)
```

Rule 14

Do not leave a space between the '/' and '=' characters when using the 'not equal to' function.

Non-graphical solutions

There is no reason why AutoLISP macros should always output some form of graphics. In the case of mathematical problems there is only need for the answer to be displayed in the screen prompt area.

The mathematical problem I have chosen to demonstrate this principle is associated with true lengths, a practical problem that is common to many geometrical problems from roof intersections to surface developments.

One method is to draw the problem in three dimensions (3D), and use ATTITUDE and LIST to give the desired length. A much shorter solution for variable parameters is to run an AutoLISP macro, and then simply respond to screen prompts for the different parameters – the answer will be then displayed on the screen.

TRUEL.LSP is a parametric program for a square pyramid. See Figure 5 – the parameters concerned are:

■ Vertical height 'H'.
■ Dimension of square base 'B'.

Therefore:

$$R = \frac{B/2}{\sin \pi / 4} \text{ and } TL = \sqrt{H^2 + R^2}$$

Load and run the program TRUEL.LSP. Test the program by entering the following values:

■ Vertical height 'H' = 50.
■ Dimension of square base 'B' = 25.

This should return a value of 53.03 (the last function in the program). Now test the program by drawing the graphics:

1. In the WCS draw a square, each side 25 units long.
2. Use the POINT command with 'x' and 'y' coordinates at the mid points of sides of the square, and a 'z' value of 50.
3. Set a VPOINT at '1,–1,1' and draw a line from this point to any intersection of the square.
4. LIST the last entity and note the length value.

TRUEL.LSP

```
(DEFUN C:TRUEL () ;NOTE: NAME OF FUCTION = FILE NAME
  (SETQ H (GETREAL "\nPLEASE ENTER THE VERTICAL HEIGHT ")
        B (GETREAL "\nENTER THE PYRAMID BASE SIZE (SQUARE) ")
        R (/(/ B 2)(SIN (/ PI 4)))
        TL (SQRT (+ (* H H)(* R R)))
  )
)
```

Figure 5

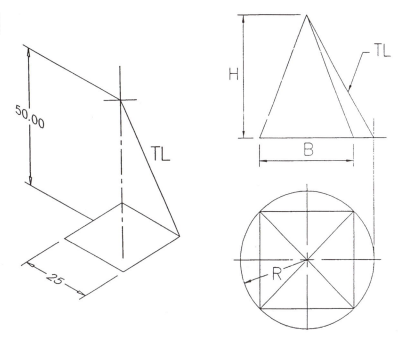

Testing input

When you compare many published AutoLISP programs with ours, you will notice the absence of any user input controls. This is satisfactory as long as our assumption of the user's competence is correct.

As you extend your knowledge of AutoLISP programming you should try to inhibit the user from incorrect input values by building checks into the program. These input checks can also be used in a positive way when looking for key words to detect the required end of loops.

Rule 15

Always use input controls when other people are to use your AutoLISP program.

In 1995 I wrote an AutoLISP program for the Science, Engineering and Technology week involving parametric design activities. I had thought that the program input requirements were self-explanatory, but – yes, you've guessed it – I had not incorporated enough input controls to satisfy the unexpected.

INITGET

INITGET is the AutoLISP function that controls the types of input allowed or disallowed by most of the GET functions. The INITGET function is placed immediately before the GET function. The GET function will then be repeated until satisfactory input is given.

The INITGET function is associated with a series of 'codes' or 'control bits' – such as '(INITGET 1)'. This would prevent the 'Enter' key being used as a response to a particular GET function (refer to the AutoLISP Manual for a list of codes).

The INITGET function also has the capability of defining key words as satisfactory input values. How often have you inputed values in ATTITUDE commands such as ARC, DIM, TEXT, etc. out of sequence, only to find that the command prompt is still waiting for a correct input before proceeding?

GETSTRING

We have already used GETSTRING in our first AutoLISP program INTRO.LSP (see page 8). What happened when you entered a space in your name?

This problem can be solved by the use of a GETSTRING 'flag'. A flag is a number that should be placed before the optional prompt (any number will do). Edit the INTRO.LSP program to include:

```
(SETQ STR1(GETSTRING 1 "PLEASE ENTER YOUR NAME: "))
```

Lets now improve our insulation AutoLISP program (INS.LSP) to incorporate a loop and an input control.

INS.LSP draws a series of shapes between two points, 'P1' and 'P2', at any given length and angle. Instead of ending the program at the completion of one line, it would be useful to be able to continue drawing a number of lines in a loop until such time as a keyboard input indicates the end of the loop.

A loop can often be broken by pressing the 'Enter' key, however, this method is of little use if you are in the middle of a program – the commands at the end of the program would not be executed.

The modified program is shown in MINS.LSP and Figure 6.

Figure 6

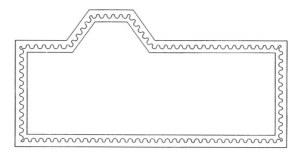

MINS.LSP

```
(DEFUN C:MINS ()
 (GRAPHSCR)
  (SETVAR "CMDECHO" 0)     ;STOP COMMAND LINE ECHOING
  (COMMAND "UCS" "W")
  (INITGET 7)
  (SETQ P1 (GETPOINT "\nPLEASE SELECT THE START POINT: "))
  (COMMAND "UCS" "O" P1)
  (SETQ P1 (LIST 0 0))
  (INITGET 7)
  (SETQ P2 (GETPOINT "\nPLEASE SELECT THE END POINT: "))
   (WHILE P2
     (SETQ D (DISTANCE P1 P2))
     (SETQ N (/ D 10)) ; 10= NOMINAL LENGTH OF SHAPE
     (SETQ NI (FIX N)) ; CREATE INTEGER
     (SETQ LE (/ D NI)) ; ACTUAL LENGTH OF SHAPE
     (SETQ Q (ANGLE P1 P2))
     (SETQ Q1 (* Q (/ 180 PI))) ; ANGLE IN DEGREES
     (SETQ D1 (* 0.6 LE) D2 (* 0.4 LE) R1 (/ D1 2) D3 (+ D1 D2))
   (COMMAND "PLINE" P1 "A" "CE" (LIST R1 0) (LIST D1 0) (LIST D3 0)"")
      (COMMAND "ROTATE" "L" "" P1 Q1)
      (COMMAND "UCS" "Z" Q1)
      (COMMAND "ARRAY" "L" "" "R" 1 NI LE)
      (COMMAND "UCS" "Z" (- Q1))
      (SETQ P1 P2)
      (COMMAND "UCS" "O" P1)
      (SETQ P1 (LIST 0 0))
      (INITGET 7 "E")
      (SETQ P2 (GETPOINT "\nENTER NEXT POINT or E for End: "))
      (IF (= P2 "E")(SETQ P2 NIL))
   )
      (COMMAND "UCS" "W")
)
```

■ (SETVAR "CMDECHO" 0) – The SETVAR function lets you change all but the 'read only' variables. I am sure that you have noticed the AutoLISP program being echoed in the prompt area of the screen. When you set 'CMDECHO' to 0, this echoing will be switched off.

▪ **(INITGET 7)** – This is the same as '(INITGET (+ 1 2 4))' and helps to 'idiot-proof' your program. The codes 1, 2 and 4 have the following effect:

1 = Stops 'Enter' being pressed
2 = Zero not allowed
4 = No negative value

Not all GET functions have the same code options as above. There are also more codes than I have shown above. (Must leave something for another day!)

▪ **(INITGET 7 "E")** – The first thing to remember is that any key words or letters such as 'E' *must* have both double quotation marks or you will get an error message. The program will be 'true' for 'P2' as long as points are entered, the loops can only be broken by entering 'E' at the keyboard. The IF function then makes 'P2' no longer true by giving 'P2' the value NIL; the program continues to its completion. (INITGET is often associated with the function GETKWORD).

At the command prompt:

```
(LOAD "MINS")
```

Test the program for loop activities. Take care when the OSNAP node is set to a value. Test the program without any OSNAP nodes set; if they are needed during the program you can enter them from the keyboard in the normal manner.

Having an argument

Brief mention has already been made to the use of global and local variables. If, as we have done so far, we simply use, for example, '(DEFUN C:CONE () ...)', all the variables we use in the program are global and do not lose their value when the program ends. Another option is to include the variable within the parentheses. This means that the variable is set up to receive a value passed to it from outside the program. This is known as 'passing an argument'.

As an example of 'passing an argument' we will use the often needed programs that convert degrees to radians, and vice versa. Enter the following:

```
(DEFUN R2D (RADS) ; radians to degrees
   (/ (* RADS 180.0) PI)
)


(DEFUN D2R (DEGS) ; degrees to radians
   (/ (* DEGS PI) 180.0)
)
```

Notice that no 'C:' prefix has been used in the above programs, as this is not done when passing an argument.

Load the programs in the usual way and test them by entering:

```
(R2D 1)
```

This should return a value of 57.2958, which is the number of degrees in one radian. Try also:

```
(D2R 57.2958)
```

This should return a value of 1.0.

You can name the functions and arguments anything you like within reason.

Rule 16

Avoid using any names resembling an AutoCAD command or any previous function.

Now let's try to incorporate these standard functions into an AutoLISP program. The basic idea is to break the program down into small common units that can be used in different programs as subroutines.

Edit MINS.LSP as follows:

```
(SETQ Q (ANGLE P1 P2))  to  (SETQ RADS (ANGLE P1 P2))
(SETQ Q1 (* Q(/ 180 PI)))  to  (SETQ Q1 (R2D RADS))
```

Load and test the program (remember that the R2D function must be in memory).

Notice how the radians to degrees function is passed an argument from within the MINS.LSP program.

You should really include your R2D and D2R AutoLISP programs in the ACAD.LSP file once they have been tested. The ACAD.LSP file is usually loaded whenever you enter the drawing editor, in this way your favourite AutoLISP macros are loaded automatically.

Rule 17

Only include in the ACAD.LSP file AutoLISP files that are used on a regular basis.

Nested loops

Nesting loops helps to reduce the length of a program and involves placing one loop inside another loop. There is no limit to the depth of nesting or the number of loops situated within each other, but the important thing to remember is that the individual loops must *not* 'overlap' each other. Think of nested loops as activities working from the inside to the outside.

The example I have chosen is NEST.LSP which draws a 'shell' graphic, which has a different number of pre-determined vectors on the top and bottom halves of a circle – see Figure 7.

NEST.LSP

```
(DEFUN C:NEST ()
  (SETQ R 100 L 6)
  (SETQ A (/ PI L))
  (SETQ P1 (LIST R 0))
   (REPEAT 2                 ;Start of first loop
    (REPEAT L                ;Start of second loop
     (SETQ X (* R (COS A)))
     (SETQ Y (* R (SIN A)))
     (SETQ P2 (LIST X Y))
      (COMMAND "LINE" P1 P2 "")
      (SETQ P1 P2)
      (SETQ A (+ A (/ PI L)))
    )                        ;End of second loop
   (SETQ L 3)
   (SETQ A (+ PI (/ PI L)))
   )                         ;End of first loop
)
```

Note how the REPEAT loops are situated within each other. This causes the primary loop to repeat twice, once for the top semicircle (six lines) and once for the lower semicircle (three lines), thus reducing the length of the program.

Figure 7

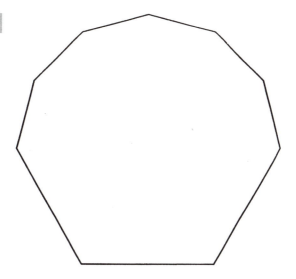

Load NEST.LSP and test the program by placing the UCS origin in the centre of the screen. When satisfactory modify the NEST.LSP program to locate the UCS origin in a chosen position returning to the previous UCS location at the end of the program.

Rule 18

You can nest as many loops as you like, one within another, but at no time must the loops overlap.

The program NEST3.LSP is a little bit of fun designed to show how to nest loops 'three deep' (see Figure 8).

Figure 8

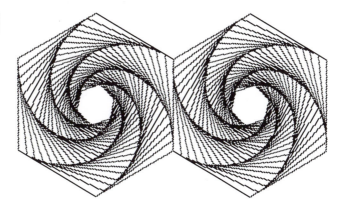

NEST3.LSP

```
(DEFUN C:NEST3 ()
 (GRAPHSCR)
 (SETVAR "CMDECHO" 0)
 (SETQ P1 (GETPOINT"\nPLEASE PICK THE CENTRE OF THE SCREEN "))
  (REPEAT 2                        ;Start of first loop
    (SETQ R 100 S 0 C 1)
    (SETQ A (/ PI 3))
    (COMMAND "UCS" "O" P1)
    (SETQ P1 (LIST 0 0))
     (REPEAT 30                     ;Start of second loop
       (SETQ XS (* R (COS S)))
       (SETQ YS (* R (SIN S)))
       (SETQ P1 (LIST XS YS))       ;Start position for hexagon
        (REPEAT 6                    ;Start of third loop
          (SETQ X (* R (COS (+ A S))))
          (SETQ Y (* R (SIN (+ A S))))
          (SETQ P2 (LIST X Y))
          (COMMAND "LINE" P1 P2 "")
          (SETQ A (+ A (/ PI 3)))
          (SETQ P1 P2)
        )                           ;End of third loop
       (SETQ S (+ S 0.1))
       (SETQ R (* R 0.95))
       (SETQ C (+ C 1))
       (IF (> C 7)(SETQ C 1))
       (COMMAND "COLOUR" C)
     )                              ;End of second loop
    (SETQ P1 (LIST 0 0))
    (COMMAND "UCS" "O" (POLAR P1 (/ PI 6) 173.205))
  )                                 ;End of first loop
  (COMMAND "COLOUR" 7)              ;Return colour to white
 (COMMAND "UCS" "W")
)
```

Note the way that the program is indented to help identify the three loops. Work from the centre outwards when trying to read the program.

- **Loop 3** – Draws six lines (one line repeated six times) in different positions to create a polygon.
- **Loop 2** – Changes the dimension of the polygon ('R'), the colour ('C') and the rotation angle ('S'). The program repeatedly returns to Loop 3 to continue the creation of a polygon (30 times).
- **Loop 1** – This re-establishes the value of 'P1' and the UCS origin and returns to repeat the above.

Modify NEST3.LSP to make both sets of polygons identical in their colour sequence.

Menu control

When using the AutoLISP macros it may be convenient to have the necessary associated screen menus automatically paged to the screen in the same way as certain AutoCAD commands operate.

The MENUCMD function controls the display of screen menus. Modify the program MINS.LSP to include (at line three):

```
(MENUCMD "S=OSNAP")
```

This will cause the '**SNAP' sub-menu of the '***SCREEN' menu to be displayed in the menu area of the screen (if the menu is enabled).

Your AutoLISP macros can control all aspects of the screen and 'pop-up' (or 'pull-down') sections of the menu.

Menu files

When reading the ACAD.MNU file you can't fail to recognise the value of AutoLISP within the menu structure. You can incorporate AutoLISP macros within the screen, tablet or pull-down sections of the menu file. Certain companies have dedicated menus for specific activities or customers, with all the special AutoLISP macros available with a single pick from the screen or tablet.

All that is required to use your own menu is to enter the menu file name (this does not have to be 'ACAD' but must have the extension '.MNU') at the command prompt.

Take care when editing the ACAD.MNU file to use a large enough word processor in ASCII or non-document mode. Remember that with certain releases of AutoCAD you will need to delete the compiled menu file (the MNX file) after every editing session. This forces the new or edited MNU file to be read, resulting in a new compiled file.

Let us return to our first graphical macro to demonstrate menu applications. Use the REC.LSP file to create a rectangle having a unit breadth and depth and save the drawing as A:RECT.DWG.

Block insertion presets

There is no need to edit the large ACAD.MNU file – let's create our own menu. Use a text editor to enter the following (remember this is only an example) – save the file as 'OUR.MNU':

```
***SCREEN
[===OUR==]
[AutoLISP]
[PROGRAMS]
[========]
[BREADTH]^C^C^P(SETQ BR ⏎
       (GETREAL "ENTER RECTANGLE BREADTH: "))
[DEPTH]^C^C^P(SETQ DE ⏎
       (GETREAL "ENTER RECTANGLE DEPTH: "))
[RECTANGL]^C^CINSERT A:RECT XScale !BR YScale !DE \;
```

Note the use of the backslash '\' and the semi-colon in the '[RECTANGL]' code.

The above code would insert the block 'A:RECT', scaling its 'Y' axis to the value of variable 'DE'. Note how the AutoLISP variables are used within the AutoCAD INSERT command.

Load and run the command by first entering, at the command prompt:

```
MENU
Type A:OUR
Then DIR A:
```

Note the compiled file. If you experience any problems with your file menu check that there are only single spaces between items requiring an 'Enter' key-press; alternatively replace each space with a semi-colon such as:

```
^C^CINSERT;A:RECT;XSCALE;!BR;YSCALE;!DE;
```

You don't really have to place a semi-colon at the end of the line as AutoCAD automatically assumes there should be one.

As this series of activities is based upon the introductory *AutoLISP in Action* topics I will resist the temptation to trespass into territory covered by other courses such as parametrics.

Return to our TRUEL.LSP program. Instead of loading the file from the keyboard modify OUR.MNU to make the macro available from a single screen pick.

```
***SCREEN
[===OUR==]
[AutoLISP]
[PROGRAMS]
[========]
```

```
[BREADTH]^C^C^P(SETQ BR ←
          (GETREAL "ENTER RECTANGLE BREADTH: "))
[DEPTH]^C^C^P(SETQ DE ←
          (GETREAL "ENTER RECTANGLE DEPTH: "))
[RECTANGL]^C^CINSERT A:RECT XScale !BR YScale !DE \;
[========]
[TRUELTHS]^C^C^P(IF(NOT TRUEL) (LOAD "A:TRUEL"));TRUEL;
```

Recompile the menu file (delete the existing MNX file) and test the menu by picking 'TRUELTHS'.

Instead of accessing the AutoLISP file from the disk drive as above, it is possible to include the entire routine in the menu file. However, this is not recommended for long programs. In AutoCAD Release 12 (and later releases) these lengthy AutoLISP files should be included in a file containing the same name as the menu file but with the extension 'MNL'. This will avoid the need to load a very large MNU file every time you wish to edit an AutoLISP file included in the MNU file.

There are four basic menu files. We will concentrate upon three different menu files to illustrate the process involved when loading a menu file (see Figure 9).

Figure 9

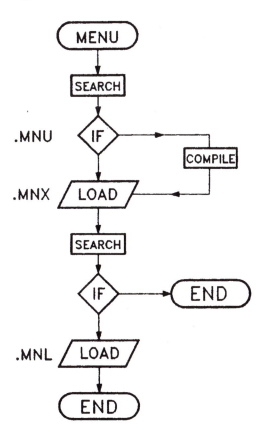

1. Search for the 'MNU' file extension in the current directory, followed by the AutoCAD directory.
2. If there is a MNU file then search for a MNX file having the same name. If there is no MNX file (or the MNX file has an older date) compile the MNU file. Load the new MNX file into memory.
3. If the MNX file has been loaded then search for a MNL file having the same name as the MNU and MNX files. If a MNL is found then load it into memory.

AutoLISP from a menu

The '[===box==]' code demonstrates the use of AutoLISP from within the menu file and is similar to the previous REC.LSP file:

```
***SCREEN
[===OUR==]
[AutoLISP]
[PROGRAMS]
[========]
[BREADTH]^C^C^P(SETQ BR ⏎
        (GETREAL "ENTER RECTANGLE BREADTH: "))
[DEPTH]^C^C^P(SETQ DE ⏎
        (GETREAL "ENTER RECTANGLE DEPTH: "))
[RECTANGL]^C^CINSERT A:RECT XScale !BR YScale !DE \;
[========]
[TRUELTHS]^C^C^P(IF(NOT TRUEL) (LOAD "A:TRUEL"));TRUEL;
[===BOX==]^C^C^P(SETQ A ⏎
        (GETPOINT "ENTER THE FIRST CORNER: "));\+
(SETQ B (GETPOINT ⏎
        "ENTER THE OPPOSITE CORNER: "));\+
PLINE !A (LIST(CAR A) (CADR B))⏎
        !B (LIST(CAR B) (CADR A)) C;
```

Load the menu (remember to delete the previous MNX file if necessary) and test the file by picking 'BOX' from the screen menu and following the screen prompts.

If you experience problems, check the spaces and semi-colons; both have the same effect, that of an 'Enter' key-press. The plus sign at the end of lines of code indicates that the program continues on another line. This stops AutoCAD from automatically including an 'Enter' key-press at the end of the line.

Standard AutoCAD commands

There is no reason why the OUR.MNU file should not contain standard AutoCAD commands. Two transparent commands I find especially useful are

the ZOOM W (zooms the drawing to include all of the detail on screen) and
ZOOM P (which zooms the drawing back to the previous zoom setting).
These transparent menu commands can be accessed whilst you are already
using another AutoCAD command (very helpful when in selection mode).
Edit OUR.MNU as follows:

```
***SCREEN
[===OUR==]
[AutoLISP]
[PROGRAMS]
[========]
[BREADTH]^C^C^P(SETQ BR ⏎
        (GETREAL "ENTER RECTANGLE BREADTH: "))
[DEPTH]^C^C^P(SETQ DE ⏎
        (GETREAL "ENTER RECTANGLE DEPTH: "))
[RECTANGL]^C^CINSERT A:RECT XScale !BR YScale !DE \;
[========]
[TRUELTHS]^C^C^P(IF(NOT TRUEL)(LOAD "A:TRUEL"));TRUEL;
[===BOX==]^C^C^P(SETQ A ⏎
        (GETPOINT "ENTER THE FIRST CORNER: "));\+
(SETQ B (GETPOINT "ENTER THE OPPOSITE CORNER: "));\+
PLINE !A (LIST(CAR A) (CADR B))⏎
        !B (LIST(CAR B) (CADR A)) C;
[ZOOM=WIN]'ZOOM W
[ZOOM=PRE]'ZOOM P
```

Load the menu and test the appendage at the command prompt.

Rule 19
Do not include ^C^C before transparent commands.

Try extending the menu title items beyond eight characters (between the
square brackets) and investigate the effect.

Drawing database

As this is an introductory course in AutoLISP we must move on to other things (despite customisation of menus being very useful). No such course would be complete without a look at the drawing database and the way in which AutoCAD stores data on graphical entities or objects.

Let's start at the deep end to get a taste for the subject:

1. Draw a line in the drawing editor.
2. At the command prompt: `(SETQ A (ENTGET(ENTLAST)))`
3. Draw an arc.
4. At the command prompt: `(SETQ B (ENTGET(ENTLAST)))`
5. Draw a circle.
6. At the command prompt: `(SETQ C (ENTGET(ENTLAST)))`
7. At the command prompt: `!A` *Use F1 or F2 to toggle the text screen*
8. At the command prompt: `!B`
9. At the command prompt: `!C`

This example shows how AutoCAD stores data on graphical entities. Each entity in the associated list between parentheses is connected to a special code or tag. Note the unique number attached to the graphical entity. This enables us to locate specific data for further use. At the command prompt:

`DXFOUT` *Select the three entities*
Name the file `A:TEST`
Type `A:TEST.DXF` *(Ref.: ACAD.PGP file)*

Note the way in which this file format uses the tag to attach specific values, similar to the drawing database.

Now lets take a close look at the drawing database. The above line, arc and circle are described as 'entities'. We are told that in AutoCAD Release 13 these entities become 'objects'. However, with such functions as ENTSEL, ENTGET, ENTLAST, ENTNEXT, ENTSEL, ENTDEL, etc. there appears to be a lack of consistency in this statement.

Information on single entities is usually obtained via the following two functions: ENTSEL and ENTGET. At the command prompt enter:

`(SETQ A2 (ENTSEL))`

Pick any point on the line. This returns the entity name and a coordinate value; this coordinate is the pick point. Enter:

```
(SETQ A3 (CAR A2))
```

This returns only the entity name. How would you extract the coordinates only? Try entering:

```
(SET A4 (ENTGET A3))
```

This returns the associated list for the selected entity ('A2') allowing access to the drawing database.

It is possible to obtain information on a group or set of entities by using the SSGET function ('SS' stands for 'selection set'). With this function there is the option to filter out certain attributes and conditions by matching them with the entire database for that particular drawing. For example, we may wish to collect information on all the circles drawn on a particular layer. Consult the manual for a complete list of filters. At the command prompt:

```
(SETQ A5 (SSGET "X"))
```

This will select all three entities in the drawing. The 'X' filter causes a search of the entire database. Enter:

```
(SETQ A6 (SSGET "X" (LIST (CONS 1 "LINE"))))
```

The SSGET function searches the entire drawing database, selecting only those matching objects (that is, only the LINE entities) – this should in this case result in a single entity. Check for a single entity with:

```
(SETQ NUM (SSLENGTH A6))
```

The SSLENGTH function determines the number of entities in the selection set ('A6').

The above CONS function is used to create a 'dotted pair': '(0 . "LINE")', as used in the associated list. There are many different types of filters available with the SSGET function that we will use at a later date.

Having selected our entities or objects, what can we do with this information?

Firstly we need to understand the dotted pairs by remembering the code or tag.

(-1 . ?)	Entity name associated with the '−1' code (unique number)
(0 . ?)	Entity type associated with the '0' code such as line, arc, circle, etc.
(8 . ?)	The '8' code refers to the layer name
(10 . ?)	The start coordinates of a line
(11 . ?)	The end coordinates of a line
(210 . ?)	The coordinate system, i.e. x,y,z = 0,0,1 in the WCS

Try to work out the dotted pairs for the arc and circle entities. (**Hints**: (i) centre point data; (ii) angle in radians (start/finish).)

Let's use our knowledge to solve a practical problem (see INT.LSP and Figure 10).

Figure 10

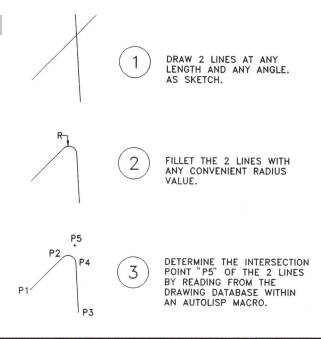

① DRAW 2 LINES AT ANY LENGTH AND ANY ANGLE. AS SKETCH.

② FILLET THE 2 LINES WITH ANY CONVENIENT RADIUS VALUE.

③ DETERMINE THE INTERSECTION POINT "P5" OF THE 2 LINES BY READING FROM THE DRAWING DATABASE WITHIN AN AUTOLISP MACRO.

INT.LSP

```
(DEFUN C:INT ()
 (GRAPHSCR)
  (SETQ A (ENTSEL "\nSELECT A LINE "))
  (SETQ A2 (CAR A))
  (SETQ A3 (ENTGET A2))
  (SETQ B (ENTSEL "\nSELECT THE REMAINING LINE "))
  (SETQ B2 (CAR B) B3 (ENTGET B2))
   (SETQ P1 (ASSOC 10 A3) P2 (ASSOC 11 A3)
        P3 (ASSOC 10 B3) P4 (ASSOC 11 B3)
   )
  (SETQ P1 (LIST (CADR P1)(CADDR P1)(CADDDR P1)))
  (SETQ P2 (LIST (CADR P2)(CADDR P2)(CADDDR P2)))
  (SETQ P3 (LIST (CADR P3)(CADDR P3)(CADDDR P3)))
  (SETQ P4 (LIST (CADR P4)(CADDR P4)(CADDDR P4)))
   (SETQ P5 (INTERS P1 P2 P3 P4 nil))
)
```

The INTERS function calculates the point where two lines intersect (see Figure 11).

In case the two lines do not intersect the argument NIL is included after the four points of the line. Note also the use of the CADR, CADDR and

Figure 11

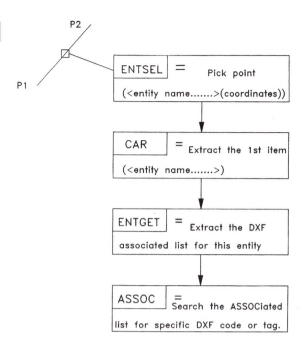

CADDDR functions – used to extract the coordinate values of the list by omitting the first entity, i.e. the code or tag. (This is not the best function to use but is appropriate at this stage.)

Test the program with:

`!P5` *and* `LINE !P5`

'Vee-slides' (see Figure 12) present practical problems requiring a high degree of accuracy based upon 'sharp corners' geometry.

Figure 12

VEE–SLIDE

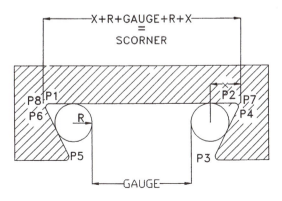

Consider manufacturing the female part of the vee-slide with roller measurements using the above system of reading the database to help establish roller measurements. Don't use 'VSLIDE' as your new function name as this is an AutoCAD command. Note how the first item from a list can be removed with the CDR function (see SLIDE.LSP). This is much easier than constructing a list with CADR, CADDR and CADDDR functions (used in INT.LSP).

SLIDE.LSP

```
(DEFUN C:SLIDE ()
 (GRAPHSCR)
  (SETQ A (ENTSEL "SELECT THE LONG LINE ")
        A2 (CAR A) A3 (ENTGET A2)
        B (ENTSEL "SELECT AN ANGLE FACE ")
        B2 (CAR B) B3 (ENTGET B2)
        C (ENTSEL "SELECT THE OTHER ANGLE FACE ")
        C2 (CAR C) C3 (ENTGET C2)
        P1 (CDR (ASSOC 10 A3))
        P2 (CDR (ASSOC 11 A3))
        P3 (CDR (ASSOC 10 B3))
        P4 (CDR (ASSOC 11 B3))
        P5 (CDR (ASSOC 10 C3))
        P6 (CDR (ASSOC 11 C3))
        P7 (INTERS P1 P2 P3 P4 nil)
        P8 (INTERS P1 P2 P5 P6 nil)
  )
    (SETQ R (/ (GETREAL "ENTER THE ROLLER DIA: ") 2))
    (SETQ X (/ (* R (COS (/ PI 6)))(SIN (/ PI 6))))
    (SETQ SCORNER (DISTANCE P7 P8))
    (SETQ GAUGE (- SCORNER (+ R R X X)))
)
```

Note the mathematical relationship:

$$\tan \alpha = \frac{\text{sine } \alpha}{\cos \alpha}$$

Test the AutoLISP program by constructing a female vee-slide with roller measurement. Run the program and check the AutoLISP value against the distance between the rollers found using AutoCAD.

Exercises

This has been only an initial look at AutoLISP, and is far from comprehensive. It is advisable to develop your own work-related AutoLISP macros after completing the following exercises. Start with simple problems, only progressing to the more advanced problems after experiencing success at a lower level.

1. Modify the insulation macro (INS.LSP) to include a PLINE with a 'W' value of 1.5.
2. Rearrange the MARC.LSP to rotate clockwise from 12 o'clock.
3. The cone development program is not quite precise, as the test condition has a tolerance of 0.035 radians. Write a program to give an exact solution. (**Hint**: Try the REPEAT function.)
4. Alter the NEST.LSP program to receive input values in response to screen prompts for the number of upper and lower vectors.
5. With reference to the 'passing an argument' function converting degrees to radians, try to write similar functions to convert temperatures from Celcius to Farenheit, and vice-versa.
6. Extend the OUR.MNU file to include some standard AutoCAD commands.
7. Re-design SLIDE.LSP to make AutoCAD 'do all the work' by eliminating the trigonometry functions. (**Hint**: Use AutoCAD commands and sub-commands within the AutoLISP macro.)
8. Identify from your work experience an activity that would benefit from an AutoLISP macro.

You can now begin to develop your AutoLISP expertise by taking the next step: Part Two *Advanced AutoLISP*.

Part Two
Advanced AutoLISP

Introduction

Part One *AutoLISP in Action* introduced a series of basic AutoLISP rules. *Advanced AutoLISP* is designed to build upon these basic rules and introduces the more advanced functions of AutoLISP by means of practical examples where possible.

With recent developments in software that help the user to create macros, there is the obvious question: Why do I need to learn AutoLISP, when all that is now required is an idea of what routine you wish to automate, and with a couple of minutes involving a number of mouse clicks to start running a new macro? (I wish it was that simple!)

There is no doubt that recent developments in software has made the creation of simple macros very easy, and has opened up a wealth of customisation and macro creation. However, when more refinement or complexity is required in your programs, a greater understanding is required. If a level of 'intelligence' is to be built into your macros, then the necessary understanding takes time to acquire.

I see no reason why both methods cannot sit side by side for the benefit of non-programmers (such as myself) whose expertise and time is reserved for the CAD process.

The understanding of most of the mathematical solutions used in this book is considerably higher than the level necessary to achieve the City & Guilds *AutoLISP Programming* competencies (C&G 4351–005) and are used simply to demonstrate the practical application of such functions.

Those wishing to restrict their studies to the above qualification need not concern themselves with the following functions used in this chapter:

```
INTERS   MAPCAR   SSADD   SSDEL   SIN   COS   ATAN
```

Part Two is designed to be a logical progression from *AutoLISP in Action*, offering solutions to the more complex practical problems faced by users of AutoCAD. The use of AutoLISP in the customisation of individual companies' systems have contributed considerably to the efficiency and quality of their organisations.

Note

There are those who think in terms of 'Auto*LIST*'! – for as you will have already noticed, everything in AutoLISP is contained within parentheses and that everything between two parentheses represents a *list*.

Types of data

Symbols

Symbols are more commonly referred to as variables which are set to contain other data types such as 'strings', 'real' numbers or 'integers', etc. These variables should have unique names starting with a letter, such as 'FILE1', 'P1', 'T1', etc.

Do not use the following names for variables as they have been reserved for other uses: 'PI', 'NIL' and 'T'. Do not use spaces, periods (.), single or double quotes (' or ") or semicolons (;) anywhere in names of your variables. 'PI' is the AutoCAD name for the mathematical constant 'π' – the ratio of a circle's circumference to its diameter. In AutoCAD it is calculated to six decimal places; however, greater accuracy is achieved when PI is used within an AutoLISP macro.

'NIL' and 'T' are used in AutoLISP as responses to checks on a particular test condition – a test condition will be either true (AutoLISP will return 'T') or not true (AutoLISP will return 'NIL').

An empty list – two parentheses with nothing between them – also has the value NIL; it has *no* value. Remember the difference between this and zero.

Lists

A 'list' may be thought of as a variable containing multiple values (or elements), for instance:

```
(6 5 4.2)  or  (x y z)
```

Atoms

An 'atom' is a variable with only one value such as "6" note the lack of parenthesis.

Strings

Any collection of alphanumeric characters enclosed within quotes (for instance a line of text) is known as a 'literal string'. Numbers can also form a string, for instance: '64.2'. However, such numbers lose their numeric value if they are not converted to a 'real' number or an 'integer' (this can be done with an AutoLISP function). Strings are regularly used as prompts.

File descriptors

File descriptors are variables containing a file name, such as '(SETQ FILEDESCRIPTOR (OPEN "AUTOEXEC.BAT "r"))'. The variable 'r' is used to open the file as a 'read only' file.

Subroutines

Internal functions, or external functions such as the 'degrees to radians' or 'radians to degrees' conversion macros (*AutoLISP in Action* – page 24), are subroutines.

Reals

'Real' numbers are numeric values with up to 14 decimal places. Values must have digits on both sides of the decimal point such as '0.5' and '3.0' (not simply '.5' or '3').

Integers

'Integers' are whole numbers (without a decimal point or any decimal places) such as 3, –700, 12345, etc.

Type testing

Start a new drawing; at the AutoCAD command prompt, enter the following:

`!A` This should return a NIL as we have not assigned any value to the variable 'A'

`!PI` Note the existing value

`!T` Note the existing value

At the command prompt enter:

```
(SETQ A "THIS IS A STRING")
```

Now try '!A' again and note the difference. Now enter:

```
(SETQ A NIL)
```

Try '!A' now; you can empty a variable by using the value 'NIL'. Now try:

```
(SETQ A (- 2 2))
```

Check '!A' again – this is the difference between zero and NIL.

The AutoLISP TYPE function returns the 'type' of the element specified within the function parentheses.

Below is a list of element types (this is not, however, a comprehensive list; see the AutoLISP Manual for others):

```
FILE   File descriptor
INT    Integer (whole number)
LIST   List
REAL   Real number
STR    String
SUBR   Subroutine
SYM    Symbol
```

To try out the TYPE function, enter at the command prompt:

```
(SETQ A 10 B 1.0 C "THIS IS FUN" D '(1 2 3))
```

Now, in turn, enter the following lines at the command prompt, each time noting the result. This exercise should clarify the different data types:

```
(TYPE A)
(TYPE B)
(TYPE C)
(TYPE D)
(TYPE 'A)
(TYPE CAR)   What type of car is this?
```

As each line is entered, so the AutoLISP program is *evaluated* one line at a time. 'Evaluation' is the key word – the evaluator takes one line of programming at a time for evaluation. Now try:

```
(LIST 6.0 8.0)
```

This returns the listed values (this is the LIST function). Try the following, noting the result:

```
(6.0 8.0)   and   '(6.0 8.0)
```

What happens when you enter the following?

```
(SETQ P (LIST 1.0 2.0))
```

This returns the listed values.

AutoLISP functions can be used within answers to AutoCAD prompts. For instance, at the command prompt:

```
LINE
FROM POINT: Enter (SETQ P2 (LIST 6.0 8.0))
TO POINT: Enter !P
```

And now try the following:

```
LINE
FROM POINT: Enter (SETQ P2 '(6.0 8.0))
TO POINT: Enter !P
```

The single quotation mark has a special purpose and is referred to as a 'transparent' command. Notice how the single quotation mark can be used within AutoLISP but not as a direct response at the AutoCAD command prompt.

We have used the SETQ function frequently in *AutoLISP in Action*, but how do the SET and SETQ functions differ? With SET the variable name must be 'quoted' as in:

```
(SET (QUOTE S) 23.46))  or  (SET 'S 23.46)
```

This is much easier, but you cannot assign a variable directly with the SET function; the following will *not* work:

```
(SET A S)  and  (SET A 'S)  and  (SET A 6)
```

Try entering the following at the command prompt:

```
(SETQ A S)
(TYPE A)
!A
(SETQ A 'S)
(TYPE A)
!A
(SET A 10)
!S
```

If you are still confused, or find this even a little complicated, then take the simple option (as I do) and use only SETQ for setting variables.

You may now be wondering when we are going to do something more practical; however, if we are going to study AutoLISP, we may as well achieve a qualification standard such as the City & Guilds *AutoLISP Programming* certificate (C&G 4351–005). So, should things become a little tedious, remember it is in a good cause.

As promised, something practical in the form of five different problems. All associated with mathematical solutions.

Problem 1

This problem involves the manufacture of punches and dies for the development of cylinders with different cutting planes (see Figure 13). The two variables are 'AL' and 'R'. Once the curve is generated, the remaining straight lines can be added using standard AutoCAD commands. If both ends of the cylinder have the same cutting plane, then mirror the developed curve.

CYL.LSP

```
(DEFUN C:CYL ()
 (GRAPHSCR)
 (SETVAR "CMDECHO" 0)
 (SETVAR "BLIPMODE" 0)
  (SETQ AL (GETREAL "\nPLEASE ENTER THE CUTTING PLANE ANGLE ")
        R (GETREAL "\nPLEASE ENTER THE CYLINDER RADIUS ")
        P1 (GETPOINT "\nPLEASE PICK THE DEVELOPMENT START POINT ")
 )
   (COMMAND "UCS" "O" P1)
    (SETQ P1 (LIST 0 0))
    (SETQ A (/ PI 90)) ;accuracy expressed as radians
     (REPEAT 180           ;accuracy
      (SETQ B (- R (* R (COS A)))
            H (/ B (COS (* (/ PI 180) AL)))
            Y (SQRT (- (* H H)(EXPT B 2)))
            X (* R A) P2 (LIST X Y)
     )
      (COMMAND "LINE" P1 P2 "" )
      (SETQ P1 P2)
      (SETQ A (+ A (/ PI 90))) ;accuracy
    )
      (COMMAND "UCS" "P")
      (SETVAR "CMDECHO" 1 )
      (SETVAR "BLIPMODE" 1)
      (PRINC)
 )
```

Figure 13

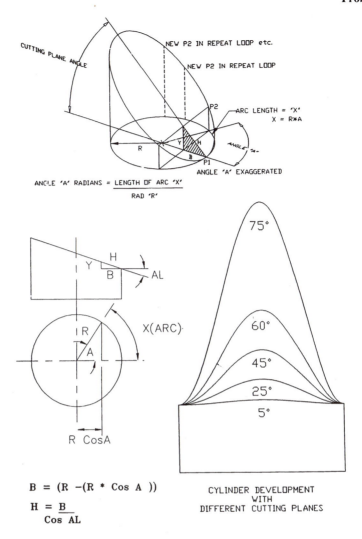

$$B = (R - (R * Cos\ A))$$

$$H = \frac{B}{Cos\ AL}$$

The above program introduces a number of new features:

- **SETVAR** – The SETVAR function enables you to set (and restore) AutoCAD system variables such as 'CMDECHO' and 'BLIPMODE'. You should really use the GETVAR function to establish the current mode, by using '(SETQ SAM (GETVAR "BLIPMODE"))'. This enables you to restore the original value at the end of your program with '(SETVAR "BLIPMODE" SAM)'.

- **CMDECHO** – Commands executed with the COMMAND function are not echoed to the screen if this system variable is set to '0' (zero). 'BLIPMODE' is toggled on and off in the same way.

Note: If you are using the 'CMDECHO' in your programs and your program 'bombs', it is helpful to be able to identify the problem line in your program. This is not possible when 'CMDECHO' is set to '0'. It is therefore better to add the line '(SETVAR "CMDECHO" 1)' to your program and change the '1' to '0' when complete. If any macro containing '(SETVAR "CMDECHO" 0) is operative in the drawing editor it is not sufficient to alter or remove this line in the program, you must also enter from the keyboard: 'SETVAR CMDECHO 1'.

In the CYL.LSP program there are three comments regarding accuracy. These three lines need editing as the radius value varies or as the need for accuracy changes:

- ▣ **SIN/COS** – These are the standard trigonometrical functions. It is very important to remember that values are expressed in radians and not degrees. AutoCAD commands use degrees, AutoLISP functions use radians. The input value 'AL' for the cutting plane angle is in degrees; notice how this has to be converted to radians when used to calculate the variable 'H'.
- ▣ **EXPT** – In *AutoLISP in Action* we used '(* A A)' to square a number (in this case the variable 'A'). I have shown two different methods when calculating the variable 'Y'. The EXPT function returns a variable raised to a specific power such as:

```
(EXPT 3.0 2.0) returns 9.0
(EXPT 2 2) returns 4
```

Load and run the program remembering to re-load the program if you edit it in any way. Test the program by inputing different parameters.

Problem 2

This program is an extension to Problem 1 and includes knowledge gained from the CONE.LSP. (See *AutoLISP in Action*, page 16.)

A manufacturer in the clothing industry is interested in the possible solution for a jacket sleeve department. What is required is an AutoLISP program that automatically generates the graphics in response to four basic input parameters (see Figure 14):

Figure 14

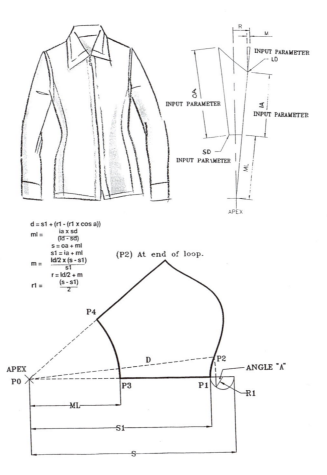

- Small diameter – 'SD'
- Large diameter – 'LD'
- Inside arm length – 'IA'
- Outside arm length – 'OA'

The resultant graphics need to be down-loaded to a 'laser' cutting machine to aid the manufacturing process.

The apex of the cone 'PO' is the origin for the construction, drawing the upper part of the sleeve ('P1' to 'P2') in a loop calculated from the apex for each different vector in the curve. One hundred vectors are used to construct the upper curve, but the value can be altered to suit the particular accuracy required. The current value of angle 'A' is then used to construct the lower arc, once more using the cone apex as its datum point. The ends of these two curves are then connected by straight lines, 'P2'–'P4' and 'P3'–'P1', to complete the curve development.

In order to download this profile to the production software for processing, the vectors should be transformed into a PLINE by the AutoCAD PEDIT command. If a seam allowance is necessary, offset this PLINE the desired value.

SLEEVE.LSP

```
(DEFUN C:SLD ()    ; SLeeve Development
 (GRAPHSCR)
 (SETVAR "BLIPMODE" 0)
 (SETVAR "CMDECHO" 0)
 (SETQ SD (GETREAL "\nPLEASE ENTER THE SMALL DIA OF SLEEVE "))
 (SETQ LD (GETREAL "\nENTER THE LARGE DIA OF SLEEVE (ARM-PIT) "))
 (SETQ IA (GETREAL "\nPLEASE ENTER THE INSIDE ARM LENGTH "))
 (SETQ OA (GETREAL "\nPLEASE ENTER THE OUTSIDE ARM LENGTH "))
 (SETQ ML (/ (* IA SD)(- LD SD)))
 (SETQ S (+ OA ML) S1 (+ IA ML))
 (SETQ M (/ (* (/ LD 2)(- S S1)) S1))
 (SETQ R (+ (/ LD 2) M) R1 (/ (- S S1) 2))
 (SETQ PO (LIST 0 0) P1 (LIST S1 0) P3 (LIST ML 0))
 (SETQ A (/ PI 50))        ; Top part of sleeve accuracy
 (COMMAND "LINE" P1 P3 "")
  (REPEAT 100             ; Construct upper part of sleeve
    (SETQ D (+ S1 (- R1 (* R1 (COS A)))))
    (SETQ X (* D (COS (* A (/ R S)))))
    (SETQ Y (* D (SIN (* A (/ R S)))))
    (SETQ P2 (LIST X Y))
    (COMMAND "LINE" P1 P2 "")
    (SETQ P1 P2)
    (SETQ A (+ A (/ PI 50)))
  )
 (SETQ X (* ML (COS (* A (/ (/ SD 2) ML)))))
 (SETQ Y (* ML (SIN (* A (/ (/ SD 2) ML)))))
```

```
(SETQ P4 (LIST X Y))        ; Construct lower part of sleeve
(COMMAND "ARC" P3 "C" PO P4)
(COMMAND "LINE" P4 P1 "")
(SETVAR "BLIPMODE" 1)
(SETVAR "CMDECHO" 1)
(PRINC)
)
```

There are no new functions in the macro, only an extension to the complexity of the maths functions. Remember that this is not a maths lesson so you do not necessarily need to understand how I have arrived at a solution as long as you understand the mechanisms of the maths functions.

Load and test the program using realistic parametric values.

Control codes

Certain characters can be used with textstrings such as '\n'. We have seen in our earlier programs that this forces the following text on to a new line (similar to TERPRI). The control characters consist of a backslash ('\') followed by a lower case letter; hence '\n' is a control code, other control codes include:

▪ \t – Tabs across a space of eight characters; for instance:

  (PRINC "NAME\tAGE")(PRINC) *returns* NAME   AGE

▪ \r – Forces a carriage return to print the next prompt string over the last one.

▪ \\ – Prints the backslash character; for instance:

  (PRINC "3\\4")(PRINC) *returns* 3\4

▪ \" – Prints a single quote character; for instance:

  (PRINC "4\"DIAM")(PRINC) *returns* 4"DIAM

▪ \[number] – Prints the character whose octal code is number given; this requires the text screen to be current:

  \253 Fractional half:

      (TEXTSCR)(PRINC "\253")(PRINC) *returns* ½

  \254 Fractional quarter:

      (TEXTSCR)(PRINC "\254")(PRINC) *returns* ¼

  \355 Diameter symbol (same as AutoCAD %%C):

      (TEXTSCR)(PRINC "\35510")(PRINC) *returns* ⌀10

\370   Degree symbol (same as AutoCAD %%D):

```
(TESTSCR)(PRINC "10\370")(PRINC)  returns  10°
```

Some more maths before returning to our practical problems: the 'equal' function:

```
(= 4 4.0)  returns  T
(= 4 4.1)  returns  NIL
(= "YES" "YES")  returns  T
(= "YES" "NO")  returns  NIL
```

For instance, type the following at the command prompt:

```
(SETQ N1 4 N2 4.1)
(EQUAL N1 N2 0.1)  returns  T
(EQUAL N1 N2 0.2)  returns  NIL
```

The 'not equal' function is the opposite; note that you should *not* leave a space between the two symbols '/' and '=':

```
(/= 4 4.1)  returns  T
(/= "YES" "YES")  returns  NIL
```

Now try the 'less than' function:

```
(< 10 20)  returns  T
(< 20 10)  returns  NIL
```

Multiple entities operate by comparing pairs in sequence from left to right:

```
(< 6 10 12)  returns  T
(< 6 10 12 12)  returns  NIL
```

The 'greater than' function operates in the opposite way to the 'less than' function.

You can use a combination of '=' and '<' or '>' to give:

```
(<= ...)  means 'less than or equal'
(>= ...)  means 'greater than or equal'
```

The 'incremental' function works like this:

```
(1+ 5)  returns  6
(1+ -15.7)  returns  -14.7
```

Beware! – do not make the common mistake of placing a space between the '1' and the '+'.

The 'decrement' function works the opposite way:

```
(1- 5)  returns  4
(1- -15.7)  returns  -16.7
```

Problem 3
Putting the spark into AutoLISP

An electrical engineer has requested help with the generation of sine curves for voltages and current, having different amplitudes and phases. I have chosen the power generated in an out-of-phase AC circuit to demonstrate the program. (See Figure 15 and ELECT.LSP below.)

ELECT.LSP

```
(DEFUN C:ELEC ()
 (GRAPHSCR)
 (SETVAR "CMDECHO" 0)
 (SETVAR "BLIPMODE" 0)
 (SETQ VM (GETREAL "\nPLEASE ENTER THE MAX. VOLTAGE "))
 (SETQ IM (GETREAL "\nPLEASE ENTER THE MAX. CURRENT "))
 (SETQ PH (GETREAL "\nENTER THE CURRENT LAG(DEG.) "))
 (SETQ PHI (/ PH (/ 180 PI)))
 (SETQ P1 (GETPOINT "\nPLEASE PICK THE GRAPH ORIGIN "))
 (COMMAND "UCS" "O" P1)
 (SETQ P1 (LIST 0 0) A (/ PI 50) P7 P1
       P2 (POLAR P1 (/ PI 2) VM)
        X (/ (DISTANCE P1 P2) 25) X2 X
       P3 (POLAR P1 (* (/ PI 2) 3) VM)
       P4 (POLAR P1 0 (* 4 VM))
       P8 (LIST 0 (* IM (SIN (- 0 PHI))))
 )
 (COMMAND "LINE" P2 P3 "" "LINE" P1 P4 "")
  (REPEAT 100                 ; ACCURACY
   (SETQ Y (* VM (SIN A))
         Y2 (* IM (SIN (- A PHI)))
   )
   (SETQ Y3 (/ (* Y Y2) (* 0.75 IM))) ; Scale value = 3/4*IM
   (SETQ P9 (LIST X Y)
         P10 (LIST X Y2) P11 (LIST X Y3)
   )
   (COMMAND "LINE" P1 P9 ""
            "LINE" P8 P10 ""
            "LINE" P7 P11 "")
```
➡

```
 (SETQ P1 P9 P8 P10 P7 P11
       A (+ A (/ PI 50)) X (+ X X2)
 )
)
(SETQ AP (* VM 0.707 IM 0.707 (COS PHI))) ; Power
(SETQ APS (/ AP (* 0.75 IM)))            ; Scale value = 3/4*IM
(SETQ P1 (LIST 0 0) P4 (POLAR P1 0 (* 4 VM)))
(SETQ P12 (LIST 0 APS) P13 (POLAR P4 (/ PI 2) APS))
(COMMAND "LINE" P12 P13 "")
(COMMAND "CHANGE" "L" "" "P" "LT" "HIDDEN" "C" "RED" "")
(SETQ STR (STRCAT "%%UPOWER= "(RTOS AP 2 2)" WATTS"))
(COMMAND "TEXT" "R" P12 (/ VM 15) "" STR) ; Alter height if reqd.
(COMMAND "UCS" "P")
(COMMAND "ZOOM" "A")
(SETVAR "CMDECHO" 1)
(SETVAR "BLIPMODE" 1)
)
```

Figure 15

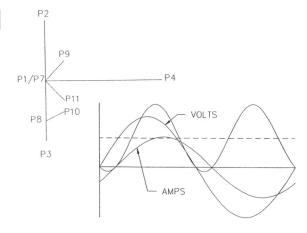

Take 'VM' and 'IM' as the maximum voltage and current; when the current is lagging the voltage by ϕ (phi):

Instantaneous voltage = VM $\times$ sin A = Y
Instantaneous current = IM $\times$ sin (A $-$ ϕ) = Y2
Instantaneous power = Y $\times$ Y2 = Y3
Power = VM (r.m.s.) $\times$ IM (r.m.s.) $\times$ cos ϕ

Notice that once more the curves are constructed by a series of vectors drawn from 'P1' to 'P9', from 'P8' to 'P10' and from 'P7' to 'P11'. The position of 'P9', 'P10' and 'P11' in the drawing are exaggerated for clarity, the actual length of each vector is governed by the accuracy required. Two new functions are used in this program:

■ **STRCAT** – Concatenates strings (ties several strings together like links in a chain); the strings are combined to make one string without spaces. For instance, enter:

```
(SETQ A "THIS" B "IS" C "FUN")
(STRCAT A B C) returns "THISISFUN"
(STRCAT A " " B " " C) returns "THIS IS FUN"
```

■ **RTOS** – Converts a length or real number into a string. The actual length or number can be a variable name that has been assigned a value by SETQ. It is possible to specify a mode and precision for the number:

Mode 1 = Scientific
Mode 2 = Decimal
Mode 3 = Feet and inches with decimals of an inch
Mode 4 = Feet and inches with fractions

For instance, enter:

```
(RTOS 112.5 2 3) returns "112.500"
(SETQ A 12.5)
(RTOS A 3 2) See if you can work this one out!
```

Before running the program make sure that the 'hidden' linetype is loaded. It is also a good idea to set the screen limits to a reasonable size, i.e. (0, 0) to (1000, 800) for a 230 V maximum voltage.

The program requests the user to input the maximum voltage and current values, including the amount of current lag. A convenient position is then selected on the screen for the graph origin, with the UCS origin temporarily set to this point as we have seen in other programs. The 'X' and 'Y' coordinate points for 'P9', 'P10' and 'P11' are then calculated relative to this new origin, with 100 vectors set to each of these three curves by means of the REPEAT function.

Note the use of the STRCAT function and the way in which the text height is made a ratio of the input value 'VM': i.e. '(/ VM 15)'.

Note also the lack of comments in the program. This is very bad practice and, as stated in *AutoLISP in Action* I have for simplicity reduced comments to the bare minimum in the expectation that you will add them to the programs.

With a power supply there is a need to satisfy certain conditions. If the power factor (cos φ) falls below 0.85, there can be a penalty imposed upon the consumer because of the need to increase the current to achieve the desired power. Hence the need for a test condition to highlight this condition (with a red flashing arrow) from within the above program.

Using the PLINE command, with the colour set to red, create a drawing of the arrow by setting a starting width of zero and an end width of 1 unit, for a line length of 0.5. Followed by a start and end width of 0.5 for a length of 0.5, resulting with an arrow of unit length. Create a WBLOCK with an insertion point at the point of the arrow and name the WBLOCK 'WARN-ING'. Make sure that the WBLOCK resides in your working directory (unless you wish to use a path command inside ELECT.LSP).

Create a new file ELECT2.LSP by transferring or copying ELECT.LSP. Delete the line '(COMMAND "UCS" "P")' and add the following lines to the program after '(COMMAND "ZOOM" "A")':

```
(IF (> PHI 0.5548)
 (PROGN
  (SETVAR "HIGHLIGHT" 0)
   (REPEAT 20
    (COMMAND "INSERT" "WARNING" P12 (/ VM 3) " " 270)
    (COMMAND "ERASE" "L" " ")
   )
  )
 )
(COMMAND "REDRAW")
(SETVAR "HIGHLIGHT" 1)
(COMMAND "UCS" "P")
```

Note the test condition for the power factor value. Note also the new function PROGN:

■ **PROGN** – The IF function is used to evaluate one 'then' expression (remember the 'if – then – else' construction); however if the test condition '(> PHI 0.5548)' evaluates as true, the PROGN function enables us to perform a series of 'then' statements. The PROGN function can be considered as a multiple 'then' function; the IF function restricted to one instruction, with the option of another instruction taking over if the test condition is not true. The other instruction is the 'else' part of the expression. Very often the 'else' part of the expression is to 'do nothing', but this is not very good programming technique (and is something for us to consider at a later date).

The program inserts and erases the red arrow WBLOCK 'WARNING' in a loop. It is also possible to give an animated effect to the arrow by changing the insertion point within the loop (something for you to try). Test the program by entering a current lag of 30°. Repeat the test using a 32° current lag, noting the results.

Problem 4
Bridging the gap

This problem involves the construction of a 'catenary' curve:

$$y = \tfrac{1}{2} (e^x + e^{-x})$$

It was the result of a request from a Humberside business man, wishing to take advantage of their famous landmark.

SUSP.LSP

```
(DEFUN C:SUSP () ;SUSPENSION BRIDGE
(GRAPHSCR)
  (SETQ L (GETREAL "\rPLEASE ENTER THE BRIDGE SPAN ")
      H (GETREAL "\rPLEASE ENTER THE HEIGHT OF THE BRIDGE ")
      X (- 0 (/ L 2)) P1 (LIST (- 0 (/ L 2)) (- H (* 0.548 H))) Q T)
  (WHILE Q
    (SETQ A (EXP (* 2 x (/ 1.0 L))) B (EXP (- 0 (* 2 x (/ 1.0 L))))
        Y (- (* 0.324 H (+ A B)) (* 0.548 H)) P2 (LIST X Y))
    (COMMAND "LINE" P1 P2 "")
    (SETQ P1 P2 X (+ x (/ L 50)))
    (IF (> x (/ L 2))(SETQ Q NIL))
  )
)
```

Figure 16

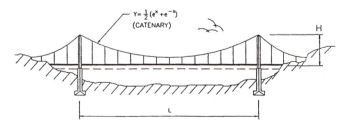

SUSPENSION BRIDGE

use SUSP LSP with an INPUT value for "H" and "L"

The program, SUSP.LSP, is only short, but introduces the new function EXP (do not confuse this with the function EXPT, and do not worry about the maths). (See Figure 16.)

▪ **EXP** – Calculates the mathematical constant 'e' (2.71828 to five decimal places) raised to the power of a real number. For instance, enter:

```
(EXP 1)    returns  2.71828
(EXP 2)    returns  7.38906
(EXP 2.2)  returns  9.02501
```

The program requests the input parameters 'H' (height) and 'L' (length) prior to drawing the curve.

Problem 5
Maths high flier

For my last maths example I would like to look at aerofoil sections. Aerofoils come in a wide variety of sections each possessing different characteristics involving complex calculations (I have chosen a simple method that everyone can follow).

Figure 17

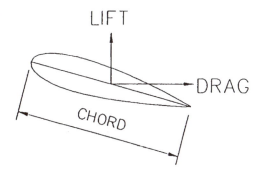

When the cross-section of an aerofoil wing is viewed parallel to the direction of motion it is called a 'profile'. The geometry of the profile depends upon certain parameters influencing its aerodynamic characteristics. However, the following simplified rules generally apply:

Thin section profiles = *Low* drag
Low lift
High speed

Thick section profiles = *High* drag
High lift
High loads
High camber

These days, the parameters of many aerofoil sections have been standardised. A very simple symmetrical profile is shown in Figure 18. A first glance at the formula is a little off-putting, but I assure you that this is much simpler than the NACA (National Advisory Council for Aeronautics USA) standard profiles.

$$Y2 = TH \left\{ \left[1.4845 \sqrt{\frac{X}{CH}} \right] - \left[0.63 \frac{X}{CH} \right] - \left[1.758 \left(\frac{X}{CH} \right)^2 \right] \right.$$

$$\left. + \left[1.4215 \left(\frac{X}{CH} \right)^3 \right] - \left[0.5075 \left(\frac{X}{CH} \right)^4 \right] \right\}$$

CH = chord length

TH = thickness of profile (maximum when X = 0.3 × CH)

Figure 18

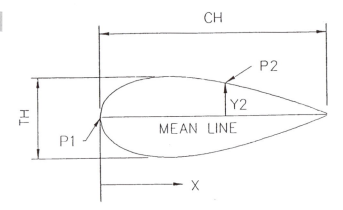

Note how the routine AEROFOIL.LSP replaces the lengthy formula for 'Y2' with 'A', 'B', 'C', 'D' and 'E'. You do not have to do this, but not only does it simplify the maths, it also makes the program easier to debug in the event of a mistake.

AEROFOIL.LSP

```
(DEFUN C:AERO ()
(GRAPHSCR)
(PROMPT "PLEASE PICK THE L.H. END OF CHORD")
(COMMAND "UCS" "O" PAUSE)
 (SETQ P1 (LIST 0 0)
       CH (GETREAL "\nPLEASE ENTER THE CHORD LENGTH ")
       TH (GETREAL "\nENTER THE MAX. PROFILE THICKNESS ")
       X (/ CH 100)) ; Accuracy of profile
  (REPEAT 100
    (SETQ A (* (SQRT (/ X CH)) 1.4845)
          B (* (/ X CH) 0.63)
          C (* (EXPT (/ X CH) 2.0) 1.758)
          D (* (EXPT (/ X CH) 3.0) 1.4215)
          E (* (EXPT (/ X CH) 4.0) 0.5075)
          Y2 (* (- (+ A D) (+ B C E)) TH)
          P2 (LIST X Y2))
```

➡

```
 (COMMAND "LINE" P1 P2 "")
 (SETQ P1 P2 X (+ X (/ CH 100)))
)
(COMMAND "MIRROR" "C" (LIST 0 0)(LIST CH TH) "" (LIST 0 0)
                  (LIST CH 0) "" "UCS" "P")
)
```

This program is a good example of the use of the EXPT function that we have already used in the CYL.LSP macro, and completes our look at problems using the maths functions. However, there is one more maths function to cover in order to satisfy the requirements of the City & Guilds *AutoLISP Programming* scheme (C&G 4351–005).

■ **REM** – The name comes from 'remainder'. This function returns the remainder of the mathematical division of one number by a second number. If the function has more than two arguments, the first is divided by the second, the corresponding remainder by the third and so on. (Do not confuse this function with the REM command in BASIC, which stands for 'remark'.)

For instance:

```
(REM 10 3)  returns 1
(REM 11.5 1.7)  returns 1.3
```

That is, $6 \times 1.7 = 10.2$, and $11.5 - 10.2 = 1.3$ (the remainder). Also:

```
(REM 20 7 4)  returns 2
```

That is, $2 \times 7 = 14$, $20 - 14 = 6$ (remainder), and $1 \times 4 = 4$, $6 - 4 = 2$ (remainder).

Subfunctions

In *AutoLISP in Action*, page 24, we were 'passing arguments' in our degrees-to-radians (and vice versa) conversion macros. How about defining the trigonometrical 'tangent' using an argument? Remember that:

Remember $\tan \alpha = \dfrac{\sin \alpha}{\cos \alpha}$

At the command prompt enter:

```
(DEFUN TAN (ANG)(/ (SIN ANG)(COS ANG))
(TAN (/ PI 4))  returns 1.0
```

Remember to use angles in radians not degrees. Check this value by looking up tables or using your calculator. Try other values if you have any doubt.

In Problem 3 we used the STRCAT function. I want now to extend our knowledge of the string function GETSTRING, but first lets link our maths with strings. Try the following:

```
(SETQ a 5)
(SETQ A 5)
(EQUAL a A) returns T
(EQUAL "a" "A") returns NIL
```

Here 'a' and 'A' are strings (upper and lower case respectively) and in order for strings to be equal they must have the same case.

■ **GETSTRING** – One of the GET family of functions used to obtain an input from the user in the form of a string. When the AutoLISP interpreter reads a GET function it stops processing the program and waits for some form of input from the user, hence the need for a screen prompt (otherwise we would not know why the computer had stopped).

Strings are series of alphanumeric characters (i.e. letters, numbers or special characters) placed in quotation marks to avoid confusing them with symbol names:

```
(PRINC "THIS IS\nGREAT FUN")(PRINC)
```
returns
```
THIS IS
GREAT FUN
```

Always remember that numbers inside strings are treated as a series of ASCII character codes. For instance: '64' does not mean 'sixty four' but the character whose ACSII *code* is '64' – that '@' symbol. (We will deal with the ASCII codes in more detail later).

```
(SETQ TXT (GETSTRING "Please enter your name"))
```

When you wrote your very first AutoLISP macro in *AutoLISP in Action* I asked the question 'What would happen if you try to use a space when you enter your name?' The problem with extra spaces can be avoided as follows:

```
(SETQ TXT (GETSTRING T "Please enter your name"))
```

When you use a 'T' flag the user can enter spaces in response to the prompt without any problems. Note that pressing the space bar does not now have the same effect as pressing the 'Enter' key.

Problem 6
Text in a string

Many years ago I was asked for a simple macro to rotate text about a common axis of rotation.

The simplest solution is to use the AutoCAD TEXT command to input one character at a time, in a loop that rotates the position of each character one increment at a time.

RT.LSP

```
(DEFUN C:RT ()
(GRAPHSCR)
 (SETQ P0 (GETPOINT "\nPLEASE PICK THE CENTRE POINT OF TEXT "))
 (COMMAND "UCS" "O" P0)
 (SETQ P0 (LIST 0 0))
 (SETQ N (GETINT "\nPLEASE ENTER THE NUMBER OF CHARACTERS "))
 (SETQ H (GETDIST "\nPLEASE ENTER THE TEXT HEIGHT "))
 (SETVAR "CMDECHO" 0)
 (SETQ R (/ (/ H 2)(SIN (/ PI N))))
 (SETQ X 0 Y R C T A 0)
 (SETQ P1 (LIST X Y))
   (REPEAT N
    (SETQ W H)
    (SETQ S (GETSTRING 1 "<ENTER> ONE CHARACTER AT A TIME "))
    (IF (EQ S "I")(SETQ W (* 0.5 H)))
    (SETQ A1 (* (+ A (/ (* 0.5 W) R)) (- 0 1) 57.296))
    (COMMAND "TEXT" P1 H A1 S)
    (SETQ A (+ A (/ W R)))
    (SETQ X (* R (SIN A)))
    (SETQ Y (* R (COS A)))
    (SETQ P1 (LIST X Y))
   )
  (COMMAND "UCS" "P")
  (SETVAR "CMDECHO" 1)
 (PRINC)
)
```

The program prompts you to enter characters, including spaces, one at a time. The program automatically calculates the arc from the number of characters required ('N') and terminates the repeat loop once the required number of characters has been entered.

Figure 19

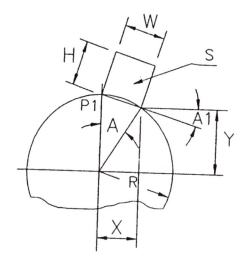

When using upper case, the letter 'I' requires a modification to the width of chord 'W' (see Figure 19). Notice how IF is used to detect the use of this character. Note also that 'A' is in radians for AutoLISP calculations, but that 'A1' is in degrees, as this variable is used within the AutoCAD TEXT command.

Figure 20

The two new functions used in this macro are EQ and GETINT. Try using GETREAL instead of GETINT when defining 'N' in the program and note the results.

■ **EQ** – Compares two expressions and checks whether or not they are identical.
■ **GETINT** – This allows only whole numbers (integers) to be entered by the user. If the input is anything other than an integer, the prompt is repeated until a whole number is entered.

Problem 7
A slant on text style

One interesting aspect concerning readers' responses to the published articles on AutoLISP in the CADuser Magazine was the interest expressed in special text macros (fuelled by Problem 6). I therefore make no excuse for another text-related problem in order to introduce you to more AutoLISP functions.

The program OBTXT.LSP draws oblique text; the characters sloping backward and forward by varying amounts, based on the input value of the number of characters in the text string. The overall included angle is 60°. The height of the text 'H' is also varied from the outside inwards to give the effect shown in Figure 21.

OBTXT.LSP

```
(DEFUN C:OBTXT () ; OBlique TeXT
(GRAPHSCR)
 (SETQ NU (GETINT "\nENTER THE NUMBER OF CHARACTERS REQUIRED ")
       H (GETDIST "\nENTER THE MAXIMUM TEXT HEIGHT ")
       P1 (GETPOINT "\nPICK THE START POINT FOR THE TEXT ")
        OB (- 30) OBINC (/ 60 (1- NU))
        COUNT 0 HINC (/ (* 0.5 H) (/ NU 2)))
 (SETVAR "CMDECHO" 0)
  (REPEAT NU
   (SETQ W H COUNT (1+ COUNT)
        S (GETSTRING 1 "\n<ENTER> THE CHARACTERS ONE AT A TIME "))
   (IF (EQ S "I")(SETQ W (* 0.5 H)))
   (COMMAND "STYLE" "" "" "" "" OB "" "" ""
           "TEXT" P1 H 0 S)
   (SETQ P1 (POLAR P1 0 W) OB (+ OB OBINC))
      (COND
           ((> COUNT (/ (FLOAT NU) 2))(SETQ H (+ H HINC)))
           ((< COUNT (/ (FLOAT NU) 2))(SETQ H (- H HINC)))
           ((= (/ COUNT (/ NU 2)) 1.0)(SETQ H H))
           (T COUNT)
      )
  )
 (COMMAND "STYLE" "" "" "" "" 0 "" "" "")
 (SETVAR "CMDECHO" 1)
 (PRINC)
)
```

Figure 21

The number of characters has to be an integer (GETINT) in order that the variable 'NU' can be used in the REPEAT loop. GETREAL would not work in the loop, as you will have noticed from Problem 6. However, the COND test condition will not work satisfactorily as an integer, as 'NU' ÷ 2 would always return an integer, even if 'NU' were odd and hence not detect the central character in the string. It is therefore necessary to use a new function FLOAT within the test condition to return a real value for 'NU' ÷ 2.

Notice how the AutoCAD command STYLE is used to automatically alter the oblique angle 'OB' for each different character, i.e. a different font style is applied to each. The height ('H') of the text controls the variable height of the characters depending upon the test conditions within the loop.

When setting the original font height, make sure that the text height is set to zero.

The new functions are:

■ **COND** – The COND function is often used in conjunction with the IF function and may be considered as a 'multiple IF' function, since several possible test conditions can be offered. The order of checking is top to bottom: the first true test condition is evaluated and the function terminates. The last line of the COND function is optional and is only evaluated if none of the test conditions are true.

■ **FLOAT** – Returns a real number, having the same value as the integer.

For instance:

```
(FLOAT 3) returns 3.0
```

The program OBTXT2.LSP is a variation on the same theme as above with the text height incremental value 'HINC' increasing towards the centre.

OBTXT2.LSP

```
(DEFUN C:OBTXT2 () ; OBlique TeXT
(GRAPHSCR)
 (SETQ NU (GETINT "\nENTER THE NUMBER OF CHARACTERS REQUIRED ")
      H (GETDIST "\nENTER THE MINIMUM TEXT HEIGHT ")
      P1 (GETPOINT "\nPICK THE START POINT FOR THE TEXT ")
       OB (- 30) OBINC (/ 60 (1- NU))
      COUNT 0 HINC (/ (* 2 H) (/ NU 2)))
 (SETVAR "CMDECHO" 0)
  (REPEAT NU
   (SETQ W H COUNT (1+ COUNT)
        S (GETSTRING 1 "\n<ENTER> THE CHARACTERS ONE AT A TIME "))
   (IF (EQ S "I")(SETQ W (* 0.5 H)))
   (COMMAND "STYLE" "" "" "" "" OB "" "" ""
           "TEXT" P1 H 0 S)
   (SETQ P1 (POLAR P1 0 W) OB (+ OB OBINC))
      (COND
          ((> COUNT (/ (FLOAT NU) 2))(SETQ H (- H HINC)))
          ((< COUNT (/ (FLOAT NU) 2))(SETQ H (+ H HINC)))
          ((= (/ COUNT (/ NU 2)) 1.0)(SETQ H H))
          (T COUNT)
      )
  )
 (COMMAND "STYLE" "" "" "" "" 0 "" "" "")
 (SETVAR "CMDECHO" 1)
 (PRINC)
)
```

Seeing that we are already dealing with angles let's now look at a useful function for obtaining angles with our AutoLISP macros.

GETANGLE

The following exercise assumes that the current AutoCAD angle units are degrees. This function pauses for an angle input by either picking two points and returning radians, or by entering a value in degrees which also returns in radians.

At the command prompt enter the following:

```
LINE
FROM POINT: pick any point
TO POINT: type @10<35.234
```

```
(GETANGLE "\nPICK ONE END OF LINE")
PICK ONE END OF LINE
END OF
SECOND POINT
END OF returns 0.614949 i.e. the angle in radians
```

```
(* (GETANGLE"\nPICK ONE END OF LINE")(/ 180 PI))
PICK ONE END OF LINE
END OF
SECOND POINT
END OF returns 35.234 i.e. the angle in degrees as you entered
```

```
(GETANGLE "ENTER VALUE")
ENTER VALUE
35.234 returns 0.614949 i.e. converts degrees to radians
```

```
(GETANGLE '(0.0 0.0) "ENTER SECOND COORDINATE ")
ENTER SECOND COORDINATE
8.168, 5.7692 returns 0.614953 (radians) – this is the
coordinate for the end of the line
```

```
(SETQ P1 (GETPOINT "PICK ONE END OF LINE"))
PICK ONE END OF LINE
END OF returns a value depending upon the location of the line on
your screen
```

```
(GETANGLE P1 "PICK THE OTHER END")
PICK THE OTHER END
END OF returns 0.614949 (radians)
```

Problem 8
A choice of layer (database revision)

Most drawings contain a series of different layers resulting in the need to constantly change from one layer to another as the drawing progresses. There are a number of useful solutions to help with this problem. I feel particularly pleased with the new solution presented by AutoCAD Release 13 for Windows.

One solution is to customise the screen menu commands to change the layer automatically as certain commands are selected. However, the request was for a quick method of changing from one layer to another by picking an object on the layer that is required.

Construct outside the drawing area of your prototype drawing a series of different lines (or even the layer names) that are constructed in the different layers (this does not have to take up much space).

SL.LSP

```
(DEFUN C:SL ()
  (GRAPHSCR)
  (SETVAR "CMDECHO" 0)
    (SETQ OB (CAR (ENTSEL "PICK AN OBJECT ON THE REQUIRED LAYER "))
          OB (ENTGET OB)
          NAME (CDR (ASSOC 8 OB))
    )
      (COMMAND "LAYER" "SET" NAME "")
      (SETVAR "CMDECHO" 1)
      (PRINC)
)
```

- ■ **LOAD "SL"** – Type 'SL' and select an object from the drawing (or the objects on the side of the prototype drawing).
- ■ **(CAR (ENTSEL ...))** – Selects the entity name or the first entity from the selected ENTSEL function.

```
(SETQ OB (CAR (ENTSEL)))
SELECT OBJECT: <Entity name: 6000004e>
```

■ **ENTGET** – Extracts the entire list for the entity name. The entity name is the first entity in the list and is a hexadecimal number representing the object: line, circle, arc, text, etc.

```
(SETQ OB (ENTGET OB))
((-1 . <Entity name: 6000004e>) (0 . "TEXT") (8 .
"TEXT") (10 245.0 175.0 0.0 40 . 4.0) (1 . "TEXT")
(50 . 0.0) (41 . 1.0) (51 . 0.0) (7 . "STANDARD")
(71) (72 . 0) (11 0.0 0.0 0.0) (210 0.0 0.0 1.0)
(73 . 0))
```

■ **CDR** – This is used to strip the first item from the associated list, i.e. '(8."TEXT")', as we did with SLIDE.LSP in *AutoLISP in Action*. Its value is assigned to the variable 'NAME'. You will see that the name of the layer is extracted:

```
(SETQ NAME (CDR(ASSOC 8 OB)))
"TEXT"
```

Some students experience difficulties with the management of entities such as the above, so let me state the procedure in its most simple terms: Select – Get – Search – Do:

1. *Select* entity or entities.
2. *Get* the entity data list.
3. *Search* for the data list associated information.
4. *Do* something.

By itself CAD will not transform a company. Unless the role of CAD is properly considered and its use is integrated into an overall company strategy, CAD is little better than an electronic draughtsman.

Vectorial integration (in CAD/CAM) is well understood by practising engineers; it is the management integration with CAD that tends to lag behind, hence the need to concentrate a little more on the management of entities. AutoLISP has the ability to not only manage vectors but to control non-graphical information in a way that benefits most companies using CAD. Remember:

Select – Get – Search – Do

Problem 9
A parts list

The problem is to create an AutoLISP program that will interrogate an assembly drawing database to:

- Determine the names of all the different parts that have been inserted in the assembly drawing.
- Print the names of the different parts at a chosen point in the drawing.

I have chosen a simple four-part assembly of a pulley block (see Figure 22) to demonstrate the solution PARTL.LSP. All the information that we require is held in a series of lists in the drawing database. Our problem is, how do we extract specific entities from these lists?

PARTL.LSP

```
(DEFUN C:PL ()
 (GRAPHSCR)
 (SETVAR "CMDECHO" 0)
   (SETQ SS (SSGET "X" (LIST (CONS 0 "INSERT")))) ; entities
   (SETQ N (SSLENGTH SS)) ; number of entities in the selection
   (SETQ INDEX 0)
   (SETQ P1 (GETPOINT "\nPLEASE PICK THE START POINT FOR PART LIST "))
    (REPEAT N
     (SETQ EL (ENTGET (SSNAME SS INDEX))); individual entities from SS
     (SETQ A (CDR (ASSOC 2 EL))) ; 2nd element ASSOCiated with dxf code 2
     (SETQ INDEX (1+ INDEX))
      (COMMAND "TEXT" P1 4.5 0 A) ; 4=TEXT HEIGHT alter to suite
      (SETQ P1 (POLAR P1 (* 1.5 PI) 6)) ; 6=TEXT space between rows
    )
    (SETVAR "CMDECHO" 1)
    (PRINC)
)
```

All entities in the list are associated with a specific DXF code (like a 'tag'). If we know this DXF code, it is possible to use this value to extract the specific entity.

Figure 22

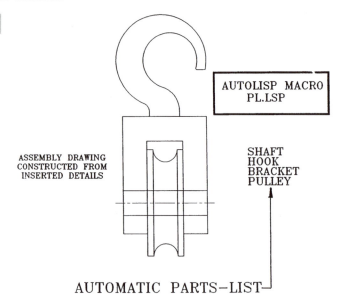

AUTOLISP MACRO
PL.LSP

ASSEMBLY DRAWING
CONSTRUCTED FROM
INSERTED DETAILS

SHAFT
HOOK
BRACKET
PULLEY

AUTOMATIC PARTS—LIST

The program incorporates some new functions:

- **SSGET "X"** – Selects from the database only those entities that match the specific criteria: '(CONS 0 "INSERT")'.
- **SSLENGTH** – This function is necessary to determine the number of items in the selection set. Once this number 'N' is determined it can then be used in the loop REPEAT function.
- **SSNAME** – From our selection set we know how many items there are, but we need to use the SSNAME function to extract the entity name for each item. For instance, if there were 50 items in the selection set 'SS' and we required the entity name of the 12 items, the syntax would be: '(SSNAME SS 11)', remember that the first item in computing is always numbered zero, hence we use 11 not 12. This is still the 'select' part of the procedure, and needs now to be followed by 'get', 'search' and 'do'.

Select
```
!SS
<Selection set: 4>
!N
4
```

Get
```
!EL
((-1 . <Entity name: 6000001a>) (0 . "INSERT") (8 .
"0") (2 . "PULLEY") (10 1 0 166.25 0.0) (41 . 0.375)
(42 . 0.375) (50 . 0.0) (43 . 0.375) (70 . 0) (71)
(44 . 0.0) (45 . 0.0) (210 0.0 0.0 1.0))
```

Search

```
!A
"PULLEY"
```

Do

```
TEXT
```

Load and run the program, selecting the point on the screen where you wish to enter the names of the parts. Test with as large an assembly drawing as possible. You may have to alter the dimensions of text in the program depending upon the size of your drawing.

Note the change in the method for use in the POLAR command, from '(* 3 (/ PI 2))' to '(* 1.5 PI)'.

Problem 10
Subentities

We are used to AutoCAD commands and subcommands, i.e. ISO is a sub-command of the ELLIPSE, and WINDOW a subcommand of all of the selection type commands. WINDOW and ISO are not primary commands, and cannot be entered directly at the AutoCAD command prompt.

In Problem 9 we extracted from the database the name of all the inserts used in an assembly drawing. Many block inserts are created with invisible attributes attached to the graphics (it is hard to justify not having attributes attached to blocks). This information can be imported to management software for post-processing with a template file. It is also possible to extract attributes by means of an AutoLISP macro should this information be required for other purposes.

AutoCAD stores the attributes as subentities of the 'INSERT' entity; such complex entities consist of a head entity with unlimited subentities, terminating with a tail (see Figure 23).

Figure 23

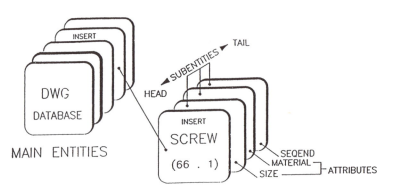

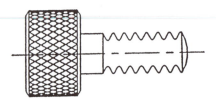

With the functions SSGET and ENTSEL the 'MAIN' entity only is returned; an ENTGET on the 'MAIN' entity will reveal the presence of attributes with the DXF group 66, code 1.

In order to access the subentities (or attributes) the ENTNEXT function is used and returns the subentity list. This list can be interrogated for attribute extraction. Repeating the ENTNEXT function in a loop will reveal all the remaining attributes (or subentities for interrogation) until the last entity or tail is denoted by the 'SEQEND' entity. The ENTNEXT function has other uses but this will suffice for the moment.

To demonstrate attribute extraction using an AutoLISP macro, I have inserted a screw with invisible attributes (see Figure 23). For simplicity I have restricted the attributes to two ('SIZE' and 'MATERIAL'); you, I am sure, will use more.

Start a new drawing, insert your WBLOCK and respond to the screen prompts. Load and run the macro ATTE.LSP. This macro will display the attributes on the screen (once you have picked the start point). You may wish to alter the text details exactly as the Problem 9.

There is no restriction to the way in which the attributes are displayed on screen (or in your drawing) – it is only limited by your programming skills.

ATTE.LSP

```
(DEFUN C:ATTE () ;Extract subentities from database
(GRAPHSCR)
 (SETQ P1 (GETPOINT "\nPICK THE START POINT FOR THE ENTITIES "))
 (SETQ SS (ENTGET (CAR (ENTSEL)))) ; Pick the screw
 (SETQ SE (ENTNEXT (CDR (ASSOC -1 SS))))
 (SETQ SS (ENTGET SE))
 (SETQ Q T)
   (WHILE Q
     (SETQ A (CDR (ASSOC 1 SS)))
     (COMMAND "TEXT" P1 5 0 A)
     (SETQ P1 (POLAR P1 (* 1.5 PI) 8))
     (SETQ SE (ENTNEXT SE))
     (SETQ SS (ENTGET SE))
     (IF (EQ "SEQEND" (CDR (ASSOC 0 SS)))(SETQ Q NIL))
   )
)
```

■ (ENTGET (CAR (ENTSEL))) – Returns the 'MAIN' entity list for the insert, in my case for the screw.

■ (ENTNEXT (CDR (ASSOC -1 SS))) – Returns the entity name of the first subentity list via DXF.

■ (ENTGET SE) – Gets the entire list of the named subentity.

■ (CDR (ASSOC 1 SS)) – Searches for the associated value for DXF code 1, i.e. the attribute, and sets the value to variable "A".

■ (ENTNEXT SE)/(ENTGET SE) – Selects and gets the next subentity list.

The condition 'SEQEND' is then tested by the IF function. If this is not the last subentity then the program repeats the while loop until such time as 'SEQEND' is detected in the subentity list, causing 'Q' to return NIL and terminating the loop.

Polylines are also complex entities, having data stored as subentities such as attributes with DXF group 66, code 1. The polyline 'VERTEX' entity (bulge or curve) is represented in the subentity list by the DXF group 42, and a secondary code that varies from 0 for a straight line to 1 for a semicircle. It is possible to enter the database and change the 'VERTEX' value, consequently changing the resultant shape of the polyline. The following problem demonstrates the use of this technique.

Problem 11

An architect has requested an AutoLISP program that will create an 'Adam' style of window as shown in Figure 24. The two parameters are the length of the major axis and the ellipse ratio (major to minor axis).

1. The construction of the ellipse presents no problems as this is a standard AutoCAD command.
2. Using ARCH.LSP, a 12-sided polygon is produced in the form of an ellipse having a major to minor axis ratio ('RA') of 1.5 (you can change this value to suit other designs). Change also the number of vectors if you wish (by altering the REPEAT loop) but modify the value of 'A' to coincide.
3. Change the polygon to a PLINE with the PEDIT command, change also the 'W' width value of the polyline.
4. Load and run the PCURVE macro and sit back in admiration.

Figure 24

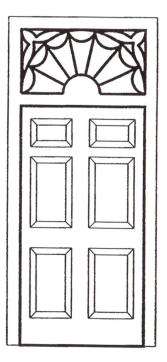

ARCH.LSP

```
(DEFUN C:ARCH ()
 (GRAPHSCR)
  (SETQ P1 (GETPOINT "\nPICK THE CENTRE OF ELLIPSE ")
         R (GETREAL "\nENTER THE MIN. RADIUS VALUE ")
  )
   (COMMAND "UCS" "O" P1)
   (SETQ P1 (LIST 0 0)
         A (- (/ PI 6)) RA 1.5
         P2 (LIST (* R RA) 0)
   )
   (REPEAT 12
    (SETQ X (* R RA (COS A)) Y (* R (SIN A))
         P3 (LIST X Y)
    )
    (COMMAND "LINE" P2 P3 "")
    (SETQ A (+ A (- (/ PI 6))) P2 P3)
   )
   (COMMAND "UCS" "P")
)
```

PCURVE.LSP

```
(DEFUN C:PCURVE ()      ;PolyCURVE
(GRAPHSCR)
 (SETQ SS(ENTGET (CAR (ENTSEL))) ; Pick the PLINE
       SE (ENTNEXT (CDR (ASSOC -1 SS)))
       SS (ENTGET SE) Q T
       CURVE (LIST (CONS 42 0.7)))
  (WHILE Q
   (SETQ SS (APPEND SS CURVE))
        (ENTMOD SS) (ENTUPD SE)
   (SETQ SE (ENTNEXT SE) SS (ENTGET SE))
   (IF (EQ "SEQEND" (CDR (ASSOC 0 SS)))(SETQ Q NIL))
  )
)
```

There are three new functions in this macro:

- **APPEND** – This function constructs a new list from two or more existing lists:

```
(APPEND '(1 2) '(3 4) '(5 6)) returns (1 2 3 4 5 6)
but try
(CONS '(1 2) '(3 4)) and note the difference
```

With APPEND both lists are combined as one, the APPEND function works only with lists and is usually used instead of CONS for building lists.

- **ENTMOD** – Updates the database.
- **ENTUPD** – This is necessary to update the image on the screen.

When the program runs, it displays each modification to the 'VERTEX' entity as it is changed in the database – change the value '(CONS 42 0.7)' and observe the effect. For a different effect, use the PCURVE macro on a standard ellipse and note the results (see Figure 25).

Figure 25

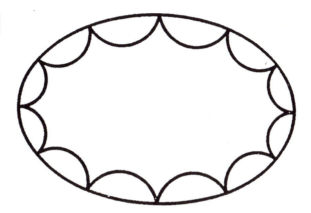

In the ATTE.LSP macro, the 'doing' part of the program (in this case the TEXT command) was executed inside the loop. It would be very useful to collect the different values for the variable within the loop but to have the doing part of the program outside the loop. This would be both more efficient in programming terms and give more control over the type of doing.

How can we collect the different results from the 'search' part of the program within a loop? Lets try to automate within a loop, the generation of a seven times table (as an example), and to direct the values for the variable 'RE' to a file for further use. We will test this idea with TEST.LSP below.

TEST.LSP

```
(DEFUN C: TEST ()
  (SETQ COUNT 1)
  (SETQ FILE (OPEN "R.TXT" "w"))
   (REPEAT 12
    (SETQ RES (* 7 COUNT))
    (SETQ RE (RTOS RES))
    (WRITE-LINE RE FILE)
    (SETQ COUNT (1+ COUNT))
    )
   (CLOSE FILE)
   (PRINC)
 )
```

Figure 26

This program uses a temporary file 'R.TXT' to store the variables, and uses some new functions:

■ **OPEN** – This function opens a file for reading or writing by using a filter: either 'r' or 'w'. They must also be enclosed within double quotation marks. If the file 'R.TXT' does not already exist, then a new file is created.

■ **WRITE LINE** – This function writes the string (and it must be a string) into the file. The string in our case is the variable 'RE' and the file is 'R.TXT'.

■ **CLOSE** – This function closes the file after use. Opened files must always be closed before leaving AutoCAD.

Having loaded and run the program (you will not observe any activity on the screen) enter:

```
TYPE R.TXT
```

This should display a row of 12 figures (the seven times table) and confirm the success of the program. Note that the DOS commands must be added to your ACAD.PGP file.

Problem 12

The problem is to extract from a drawing all the attributes data and to write this data to an external file in preparation for display in a particular format at a later date, using a single pick-point activation.

The TEST.LSP program lets us write to a file from within a loop. If we now re-visit the ATTE.LSP macro we can change the doing part of the program, from printing text on the screen to writing the same text to a file. The modified program is shown in ATTE2.LSP.

ATTE2.LSP

```
(DEFUN C:ATTE2 () ;Extract subentities from database
(GRAPHSCR)
  (SETQ FILE (OPEN "ATT.TXT" "w"))
  (SETQ SS (ENTGET (CAR (ENTSEL))))
  (SETQ SE (ENTNEXT (CDR (ASSOC -1 SS))))
  (SETQ SS (ENTGET SE))
  (SETQ Q T)
    (WHILE Q
      (SETQ A (CDR (ASSOC 1 SS)))
      (WRITE-LINE A FILE)
      (SETQ SE (ENTNEXT SE))
      (SETQ SS (ENTGET SE))
      (IF (EQ "SEQEND" (CDR (ASSOC 0 SS)))(SETQ Q NIL))
    )
  (CLOSE FILE)
  (PRINC)
)
```

1. Produce a drawing (see Figure 27) called 'Bungalow', having the attributes as shown in the invisible mode and located within the graphics (make the attributes constant for this exercise).
2. Create a WBLOCK from this drawing so that it can be used with the AutoCAD INSERT command.
3. Load and run the ATTE.LSP macro.
4. Notice that the extract file is named 'ATT.TXT'; you can change this to whatever you want.

Figure 27

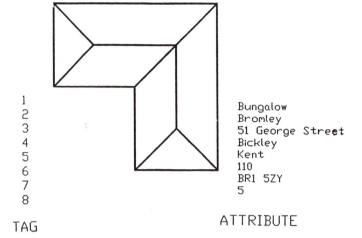

```
1
2
3
4
5
6
7
8
```

TAG

```
Bungalow
Bromley
51 George Street
Bickley
Kent
110
BR1 5ZY
5
```

ATTRIBUTE

At the command line enter:

```
TYPE ATT.TXT
```

This should display all your attributes, line by line, in the external file. This data is now available to be read at a later date.

```
File to list: ATT.TXT
Bungalow
Bromley
51 George Street
Bickley
Kent
110
BR1 5ZY
5
```

Problem 13

I am sure you would like to draw 'knurling' as shown in Figure 28. This gives me an excuse to introduce you to a new function (the last maths function to be covered) and to remind you of the concept of nested loops discussed in *AutoLISP in Action*, page 26.

Whilst the British Standard conventional representation for diamond knurling is satisfactory for manual draughting, there is no reason to restrict such graphics when using CAD. It is therefore understandable that an AutoLISP macro for the automatic construction of diamond knurling should be requested from a major engineering company.

Figure 28

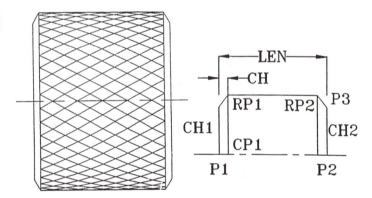

Figure 29 shows the necessary construction lines to use the macro. 'P1', 'P2' and 'P3' are then picked and the AutoLISP macro KNURL.LSP completes the remainder of the drawing.

Figure 29

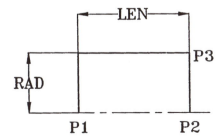

KNURL.LSP

```
(DEFUN C:KNURL ()
(GRAPHSCR)
 (SETVAR "OSMODE" 32)(SETVAR "CMDECHO" 0)
 (SETQ P1 (GETPOINT "\nPLEASE PICK THE L.H. AXIS INTERSECTION"))
 (SETQ P2 (GETPOINT "\nPLEASE PICK THE R.H. AXIS INTERSECTION"))
 (SETQ P3 (GETPOINT "\nPLEASE PICK THE TOP R.H. O/DIA OF KNURLING"))
 (SETVAR "OSMODE" 0)
  (SETQ RAD (DISTANCE P2 P3)
        CH (/ RAD (* 8 (SQRT 3))) CH1 (POLAR P1 (/ PI 2)(/ RAD 2))
        CH2 (POLAR P2 (/ PI 2)(/ RAD 2)) LEN (DISTANCE P1 P2)
        RP1 (POLAR P3 PI CH) RP2 (POLAR P3 PI (- LEN CH))
        CP1 (POLAR P1 0 CH)
  )
   (COMMAND "CHAMFER" "D" (/ RAD 8) CH "CHAMFER" CH1 RP2 "CHAMFER" CH2 RP1
        "LINE" RP2 "PERP" P1 "" "LINE" RP1 "PERP" P2 "")
   (SETQ A (/ PI 20)); ALTER VALUE FOR COARSE,MED,FINE KNURLING.
   (SETQ H (* RAD (SIN A)) TL (* H (SQRT 3))
        N (/ (- LEN (* CH 2)) TL) NI (FIX N)
        MTL (/ (- LEN (* CH 2)) NI) H2 0
   )
    (REPEAT 10 ;ALTER TO SUIT COARSE, MED,FINE VALUES ABOVE.
     (SETQ RY 0 H (* RAD (SIN A))
           H3 (- H H2) H1 (/ H3 2)
           KA (ATAN H3 MTL) K (/ H1 (SIN KA))
     )
      (REPEAT NI
       (SETQ P4 (POLAR CP1 0 RY) P5 (POLAR P4 (/ PI 2) H1)
             P6 (POLAR P5 KA K) P7 (POLAR P5 0 MTL)
             P8 (POLAR P4 0 (/ MTL 2))
       )
       (COMMAND "LINE" P5 P6 P7 P8 "C")
       (SETQ RY (+ RY MTL))
      )
      (SETQ CP1 (POLAR CP1 (/ PI 2) H3))
      (SETQ A (+ A (/ PI 20))) ; alter if above values are altered
      (SETQ H2 (+ H2 H3))
     )
  (COMMAND "MIRROR" "C" P1 P3 "" P1 P2 "")
)
```

Notice the use of OSNAP modes: 32 = 'intersection' and 0 = 'none'. Note also the new maths function:

- ■ **ATAN** – This function calculates the trigonometrical 'arctangent', i.e. returns the angle within a right-angle triangle when the adjacent and opposite sides are known.

$$\text{Arctangent } RA = \frac{H3}{MTL}$$

The value of 'H' is determined by the angle of rotation 'A' and should be altered to produce course, medium or fine knurling (see Figure 30).

Figure 30

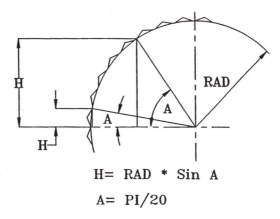

$$H = RAD * \operatorname{Sin} A$$

$$A = PI/20$$

The length ('TL') of each individual 30° diamond is also dependent upon angle 'A' and when the head size is divided by 'TL' this may not result in a whole number. Note the use of the FIX function to determine the whole number resulting in a modified length 'MTL' for the size of the diamond and the consequent need to recalculate the diamond angle 'KA' (see Figure 31).

Figure 31

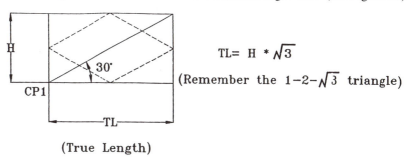

$$TL = H * \sqrt{3}$$

(Remember the $1-2-\sqrt{3}$ triangle)

(True Length)

Once the dimensions of the diamond have been established a complete row of diamonds are drawn left to right using a nested loop, followed by the re-definition of variables 'CP1', 'A' and 'H2' ('H2' was set to zero outside the loop for the first run). (See Figures 32 and 33.)

Figure 32

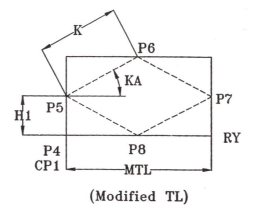

(Modified TL)

This is in preparation for the calculation of a new set of dimensions for the diamond, necessary when constructing the second row of diamonds (see Figure 33).

Figure 33

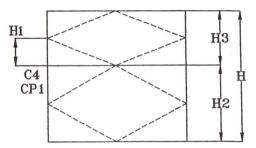

This outer loop continues to re-calculate the size of the diamonds, drawing rows that continually decrease in height until one half (or $\pi/2$ in radians) of the knurl is complete. The top half of the drawing is then mirrored, completing the drawing.

Load and run the program. This program could be improved by having the initial outline ('P1' to 'P2' to 'P3', etc.) drawn automatically from input values for length and radius (a little problem for you to solve).

The program KNURL2.LSP (see Figure 34) is an interesting variation on a theme of knurling. The shape of each diamond is created by a series of solid triangles instead of a series of straight lines. Compare KNURL.LSP with KNURL2.LSP: you will see the similarity (and the addition of seven new lines). Make sure that the FILLMODE is set to 'on' before testing the program.

KNURL2.LSP

```
(DEFUN C:KNURL2 ()
(GRAPHSCR)
 (SETVAR "OSMODE" 32)(SETVAR "CMDECHO" 0)
 (SETQ P1 (GETPOINT "\nPLEASE PICK THE L.H. AXIS INTERSECTION"))
 (SETQ P2 (GETPOINT "\nPLEASE PICK THE R.H. AXIS INTERSECTION"))
 (SETQ P3 (GETPOINT "\nPLEASE PICK THE TOP R.H. O/DIA OF KNURLING"))
 (SETVAR "OSMODE" 0)
  (SETQ RAD (DISTANCE P2 P3)
        CH (/ RAD (* 8 (SQRT 3))) CH1 (POLAR P1 (/ PI 2)(/ RAD 2))
        CH2 (POLAR P2 (/ PI 2)(/ RAD 2)) LEN (DISTANCE P1 P2)
        RP1 (POLAR P3 PI CH) RP2 (POLAR P3 PI (- LEN CH))
        CP1 (POLAR P1 0 CH)
  )
   (COMMAND "CHAMFER" "D" (/ RAD 8) CH "CHAMFER" CH1 RP2 "CHAMFER" CH2 RP1
        "LINE" RP2 "PERP" P1 "" "LINE" RP1 "PERP" P2 "")
    (SETQ A (/ PI 20)); ALTER VALUE FOR COARSE,MED,FINE KNURLING.    ➡
```

```
     (SETQ H (* RAD (SIN A)) TL (* H (SQRT 3))
          N (/ (- LEN (* CH 2)) TL) NI (FIX N)
          MTL (/ (- LEN (* CH 2)) NI) H2 0
     )
     (REPEAT 10 ;ALTER TO SUIT COARSE, MED,FINE VALUES ABOVE.
      (SETQ RY 0 H (* RAD (SIN A))
            H3 (- H H2) H1 (/ H3 2)
            KA (ATAN H3 MTL) K (/ H1 (SIN KA))
      )
      (REPEAT NI
       (SETQ P4 (POLAR CP1 0 RY) P5 (POLAR P4 (/ PI 2) H1)
             P6 (POLAR P5 KA K) P7 (POLAR P5 0 MTL)
             P8 (POLAR P4 0 (/ MTL 2))
             P9 (POLAR P5 0 (/ MTL 2))
             P10 (POLAR P6 PI (/ MTL 2))
             P11 (POLAR P4 0 MTL)
       )
       (COMMAND "SOLID" P5 P10 P6 "" "")
       (COMMAND "SOLID" P5 P9 P8 "" "")
       (COMMAND "SOLID" P6 P9 P7 "" "")
       (COMMAND "SOLID" P8 P11 P7 "" "")
       (SETQ RY (+ RY MTL))
      )
      (SETQ CP1 (POLAR CP1 (/ PI 2) H3))
      (SETQ A (+ A (/ PI 20))) ; alter if above values are altered
      (SETQ H2 (+ H2 H3))
     )
  (COMMAND "MIRROR" "C" P1 P3 "" P1 P2 "")
)
```

Figure 34

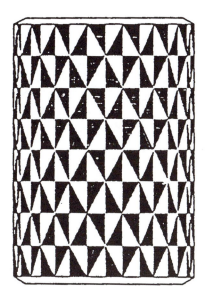

More 'doing'

All the programs to date involving some form of graphics drawn from within a loop, have had the 'doing' part of the program inside the loop. Let us use CONE.LSP as an example (*AutoLISP in Action*, page 16). The doing part of the program involves drawing a series of vectors one at a time: '(COMMAND "LINE" P5 P4"")'. The command LINE is therefore opened and closed every time the loop is repeated.

It would be far more efficient if we could collect the information for each individual point ('P5' and 'P4') within the loop and build up a long list of these points. In this way we could have the doing part of the program outside the loop so that the command LINE is opened and closed once only to construct the required curve.

The program CONE2.LSP illustrates how we can change CONE.LSP – the changes have been underlined.

CONE2.LSP

```
(DEFUN C:CONE2 ()
 (GRAPHSCR)
  (SETVAR "CMDECHO" 0)
  (SETVAR "BLIPMODE" 0)
  (SETQ R (GETDIST "\nPLEASE ENTER THE CONE RADIUS: ")
        H (GETDIST "\nPLEASE ENTER THE HEIGHT OF CONE: ")
        P1 (GETPOINT "\nPLEASE PICK THE APEX OF CONE: "))
  (COMMAND "UCS" "O" P1)
   (SETQ P1 (LIST 0 0) P2 (LIST R (- H))
         P3 (LIST (- R)(- H)) D (DISTANCE P1 P2)
         P5 (POLAR P1 0 D) PTS NIL PTS (CONS P5 PTS)
   )
  (COMMAND "LINE" P5 P1 P2 P3 P1 "") ;DRAW THE CONE.
  (SETQ RA (/ (* 2 PI R) D) A 0.035 I "T")
   (WHILE I
    (SETQ P4 (POLAR P1 A D)
          PTS (CONS P4 PTS)
          P5 P4 A (+ A 0.035)
    )
    (IF (> A RA)(SETQ I NIL))
   )
   (SETQ PTS (CONS P1 PTS)
         PTS (REVERSE PTS))
   (COMMAND "PLINE" (FOREACH P PTS (COMMAND P)))
   (SETVAR "CMDECHO" 1)
   (SETVAR "BLIPMODE" 1)
   (PRINC)
 )
```

The two new functions are FOREACH and REVERSE. All the points necessary to construct the curve are held in a list called 'PTS', however, it is necessary to empty the list prior to use with '(SETQ PTS NIL)', otherwise the list would simply extend every time you used the program.

■ CONS – This function is not new to us as we used it in Problem 9 but without explanation. The function updates a list by placing one item in front of an existing list.

The existing list in our case is 'PTS' and is always empty at the start of the program. The CONS function was also used in PL.LSP to create the special 'dotted pair' type of sublist, when the two arguments are numbers or strings. This example is different in that we are using the CONS function to build a list by adding a list to the beginning of an existing list. The first element in this case can be an atom or a list.

Once the list 'PTS' is created outside the loop, it is extended within the loop and once more towards the end of the program.

■ REVERSE – This function is easy to understand, it simply reverses a list. For instance, entering the following at the common line:

```
(REVERSE '(R O V E R (T))
```

This function is required since the list constructor CONS has created a list in the *reverse* order to that required to construct the curve.

■ FOREACH – This function works through each item in the list, one at a time, carrying out the given instruction, that is '(FOREACH P PTS (COMMAND P))'. For each item in the list 'PTS' the instruction '(COMMAND P)' is performed ('P' in our case is PLINE).

Notice the use of PLINE instead of LINE. It may be necessary to check the polyline width value before commencing the program. The use of PLINE is beneficial if such curves are to be downloaded to manufacturing software for post-processing.

Load and run the program. If satisfactory enter:

```
!PTS
```

Now that's what I call a list!

It would be a useful exercise to run both CONE.LSP and CONE2.LSP and compare the generation times for both macros. This should confirm the benefit of programming the doing part of a program outside the loop whenever possible.

In the above example we created a list prior to processing the list. What happens when the list of data already exists? I am often asked if it is possible to create the necessary graphics from a list of existing data in a spreadsheet or a database. The latest request concerned research studies involving the path of the moon over a year cycle. The data was stored in considerably large files and it was this data that had to be read to create the graphics.

Problem 14
Learning to read

We have seen how AutoLISP uses the WRITE-LINE function to write to a file (string arguments only). READ-LINE is the function to read these files; remember that AutoLISP reads ASCII files only, reading one line at a time in sequential order. The file must be open in order to read from it, and must be closed when the reading is complete.

When you open a file, you must specify the type of mode required: 'r' for read, 'w' for write, and 'a' for append; the mode definition must be typed in lower-case letters.

As an example, let us create a simple text file containing the following test data. The simplest method would be to use any non-document mode text editor; However, for practice let us use AutoLISP from the AutoCAD command prompt. The required data is as follows:

```
PTS.DAT
 32.32, 126.27
152.12,  34.80
252.10, 116.60
355.13, 120.31
360.00, 240.55
150.05, 209.36
123.36, 191.77
C
```

At the command prompt:

```
(SETQ PTS (OPEN "PTS.DAT" "W"))
(WRITE-LINE "32.32, 126.27" PTS)
(WRITE-LINE "152.12, 34.80" PTS)
(WRITE-LINE "252.10, 116.60" PTS)
(CLOSE PTS)
DIR looks in the directory for the presence of the file
(SETQ PTS (OPEN "PTS" "r")
(READ-LINE PTS) repeat, noting the results until a NIL is returned
(CLOSE PTS)
```

Now complete the PTS.DAT file.

We will now create a simple file to direct the contents of an external text file to the screen (similar to the TYPE command in DOS).

EXTREAD.LSP

```
(DEFUN C:EXTREAD ()
 (SETQ FILE (GETSTRING "ENTER EXTERNAL FILE WITH EXTENSION ")
      FH (OPEN FILE "r" ))
  (TEXTSCR)
  (PROMPT "\e[2J")
   (WHILE          ; LOOP UNTIL NIL RETURNS
    (SETQ LINE (READ-LINE FH))
    (PROMPT LINE)(TERPRI)
    )
    (CLOSE FH)
    (PRINC)
)
```

Note the use of an 'ANSI' code to clear the screen with the lower case escape character 'e'. Make sure that the following DEVICE call is in your CONFIG.SYS file:

```
DEVICE = C:\[name of your DOS directory]\ANSI.SYS
```

■ **READ-LINE** – Once a file is open, you can read each line by repeating the READ-LINE function.

Test the EXTREAD.LSP program on your PTS.DAT file. Try to locate text files outside the current directory by inserting path information in front of the name in response to the prompt 'ENTER EXTERNAL FILE WITH EXTENSION'.

So far all we have been doing is looking at or reading a file – time for more action!

The information in PTS.DAT is in fact coordinate points of a line. What is required is an AutoLISP macro that automatically reads in the data and uses this data to carry out the drawing instruction.

EXTRACT2.LSP

```
(DEFUN C:EXTRACT2 ()
 (GRAPHSCR)
  (SETQ FILE (OPEN "PTS.DAT" "r") ; OPEN FILE
       LINE (READ-LINE FILE)      ; READ THE FIRST LINE
       PTS (LIST LINE)            ; CONVERT LINE TO LIST
  )
   (WHILE LINE             ; LOOP UNTIL NIL IS RETURNED
    (SETQ LINE (READ-LINE FILE)
         PTS (CONS LINE PTS)) ; ADD NEW LINE TO LIST
    )
    (CLOSE FILE)
    (SETQ PTS (REVERSE PTS))
    (COMMAND "LINE" (FOREACH P PTS (COMMAND P)));  SEE CONE2.LSP
    (PRINC)
)
```

Note that the only test condition is WHILE; this loop terminates when 'LINE' returns NIL. If you like, you could use the test condition:

```
(IF (/= LINE NIL) (SETQ PTS (CONS LINE PTS)))
```

If, however, you do not wish to draw a line from the start point to end point of the PLINE loop (this is what the 'C' character in PTS.DAT will do) the test condition will have to detect the line containing 'C' and terminate the loop without executing this line with:

```
(IF (= LINE "C") (SETQ LINE NIL))
        (SETQ PTS (CONS LINE PTS))
```

Problem 15
A little 'releaf'

A company requested an AutoLISP macro to assist in the design of a leaf motif to be included on all their literature, and to be suitable for embroidery on to the firm's uniforms (see Figure 35).

Figure 35

The program LEAF.LSP requests an input for the horizontal length of the leaf ('LE') as well as the leaf's centre ('P1'). I have defined the end points 'P4' and 'P2' of the PLINE, instead of using the 'RAD' method (**R**adius value, **A**ngle of arc and **D**irection), so that I can relate their position in relation to angle 'A' as it rotates (see Figure 36).

Figure 36

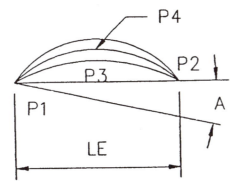

LEAF.LSP

```
(DEFUN C:LEAF ()
(GRAPHSCR)
(SETVAR "FILLMODE" 1)(SETVAR "CMDECHO" 0)
(PROMPT "\nTHE LEAF LENGTH IS THE HORIZONTAL LENGTH ")
  (SETQ LE (GETREAL "\nPLEASE ENTER THE LEAF LENGTH ")
        P1 (GETPOINT "\nPLEASE PICK THE CENTRE POINT ")
        A (- 0 (/ PI 6)))
    (REPEAT 5
     (SETQ MLE (+ LE (* LE (SIN A)))
           P2 (POLAR P1 A MLE)
           P3 (POLAR P1 A (/ MLE 2))
           P4 (POLAR P3 (+ A (/ PI 2)) (* 0.134 MLE))
           TH (* 0.07 MLE)
     )
     (COMMAND "PLINE" P1 "W" 0 TH "A" "A" -30 P4 "W" TH 0 "A" -30 P2 "")
     (COMMAND "MIRROR" P2 "" P1 P2 "")
     (SETQ A (+ A (/ PI 6)))
    )
  (SETQ P5 (POLAR P1 (* 7 (/ PI 6)) LE))
  (SETQ P6 (POLAR P1 (/ PI 4) (* 1.4 MLE)))
  (COMMAND "MIRROR" "C" P5 P6 "" P1 P2 "")
  (PRINC)
(SETVAR "CMDECHO" 1)
)
```

Note the use of a PROMPT statement prior to a request for an input value; very useful when the prompt information is lengthy.

When you have run the program, try experimenting with the value of angle 'A', along with the repeat value. Also try altering the value of 'TH' and observe the effects.

If you now try to construct a circle around the leaf design, you will notice that the length of each arm 'LE' does not fit within a circle. The same company, on receipt of the AutoLISP program, requested a leaf motif design with a circular geometry, suitable for engraving in lead crystal glass (see Figure 37).

Figure 37

The length of each arm ('LE') within the circle (see Figure 38) is found as follows:

$$LE = (OFF \times \sin A) + R^2 - (OFF \times \cos A)^2$$

This is calculated from an input value of 'R' (radius of the circle) and 'OFF' (the offset value).

LEAF2.LSP

```
(DEFUN C:LEAF2 ()
(GRAPHSCR)
(SETVAR "FILLMODE" 1)(SETVAR "CMDECHO" 0)
(PROMPT "\nOFFset = ECCENTRICITY OF LEAF CENTRE ")
  (SETQ OFF (GETREAL "\nPLEASE ENTER THE OFFSET VALUE ")
        R (GETREAL "\nPLEASE ENTER THE CIRCLE RADIUS ")
        P1 (GETPOINT "\nPLEASE PICK THE CENTRE POINT OF LEAF ")
        A (- 0 (/ PI 2))
  )
  (REPEAT 9
   (SETQ F (* (* OFF OFF)(* (COS A)(COS A)))
         LE (+ (* OFF (SIN A)) (SQRT (- (* R R) F)))
         P2 (POLAR P1 A LE)
         P3 (POLAR P1 A (/ LE 2))
         P4 (POLAR P3 (+ A (/ PI 2)) (* 0.134 LE))
         TH (* 0.07 LE)
   )
   (COMMAND "PLINE" P1 "W" 0 TH "A" "A" -30 P4 "W" TH 0 "A" -30 P2 "")
   (COMMAND "MIRROR" P2 "" P1 P2 "")
   (SETQ A (+ A (/ PI 8)))
   )
  (SETQ P5 (POLAR P1 (* 3 (/ PI 2)) R))
  (SETQ P6 (POLAR P1 (/ PI 4) (* 1.4 LE)))
  (COMMAND "MIRROR" "C" P5 P6 "" P1 P2 "")
  (PRINC)
(SETVAR "CMDECHO" 1)
)
```

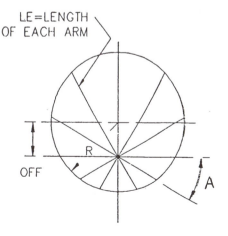

Figure 38

LE=LENGTH OF EACH ARM

R

OFF

A

The two programs LEAF.LSP and LEAF2.LSP are very similar, except for the variables 'F' and 'LE'.

$$F = (OFF \times \cos A)^2$$

Compare this with the formula for 'LE' above, which can now be simplified to:

$$LE = (OFF \times \sin A) + R^2 - F$$

Load and run the program, experimenting with variables as you did with the LEAF.LSP program.

Problem 16
AutoLISP 'cams' to the rescue

In this problem we devote our time to the design and manufacture of disk cams (see Figure 39).

Traditional methods of cam design and manufacture are, in the main, a compromise between the ideal and the practical. This often results in a cam profile modified by trial and error. However, no such problem exists when CAD/CAM processes are used.

The old workshop expression 'if they can draw it, we can make it' becomes a reality once the process is computerised.

The original request from a local university department was for a disc cam, with a knife-edge follower and having a uniform velocity as the basic motion.

Figure 40 shows the difference (for a follower rising over a 90° displacement) between the three different types of motion: uniform velocity, simple harmonic motion, and uniform acceleration and retardation. The amount of follower rise has been exaggerated to illustrate the difference.

Figure 39

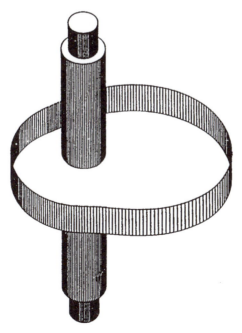

With uniform velocity (a straight-line displacement curve) the amount of follower rise is directly proportional to the amount of angular displacement. For instance: 1 mm rise in 1° rotation, 4 mm rise in 4° rotation, etc. (see Figure 40).

Figure 40

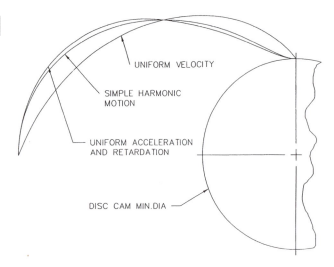

I feel sure that you could design your own AutoLISP macro for uniform velocity which is why I have included a question in the exercises at the end of *Advanced AutoLISP*.

Compare the three cam profiles in Figure 40; notice the similarity between simple harmonic motion and the uniform acceleration and retardation (which is the preferred motion in most cases). I will demonstrate the AutoLISP program using simple harmonic motion (see Figure 41).

Figure 41

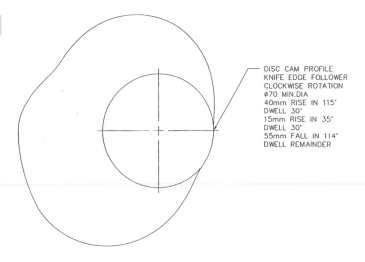

It helps with the understanding if you have previously drawn a displacement diagram. The drawing is basically a rectangle with a semi-circle drawn on any side (I prefer the left-hand side) of the rectangle. The height of the rectangle (and the diameter of the semi-circle) is 'R', which is the amount of follower rise; the length of rectangle (along its 'X' axis) can be any convenient distance. For simplicity, divide the semi-circle and rectangle length into six equal divisions (see Figure 42). (In the AutoLISP program I have used 90 equal divisions, but you can alter this number to suit the particular accuracy you require.)

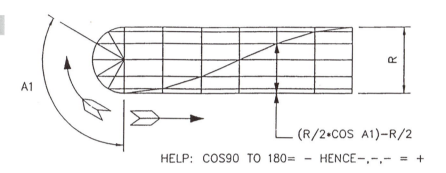

Figure 42

Extend horizontal lines from the intersection points on the semi-circle. Draw a smooth curve between all the intersection points in the rectangle starting at the bottom left-hand corner and progressing one increment at a time, that is: first semi-circle division is the first rectangular division, second semi-circle division is the second rectangular division (in the direction of the arrows shown in the Figure).

The amount of follower rise is simply the vertical distance from the base of the rectangle to the constructed curve at any angle along the 'X' axis of the rectangle:

$$\left(\frac{R}{2} \times \cos A1\right) - \frac{R}{2}$$

The convenient length for the 'X' axis is the total angle of cam displacement. If, for example, the total displacement is 90°, then the follower rise would, in the above Figure, have displacement divisions of 15°.

The distance for the follower rise can now be considered as a spoke of a wheel whose original length is equal to half of the minimum diameter, and increases in length as the spoke rotates through the displacement angle (see Figure 43).

Figure 43

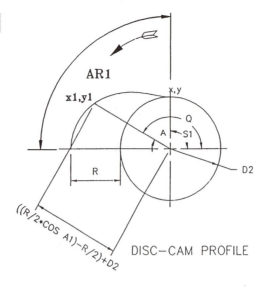

DISC—CAM PROFILE

The program SHMK.LSP is shown below.

SHMK.LSP

```
(DEFUN C:SHMK () ;SIMPLE HARMONIC MOTION, KNIFE EDGE FOLLOWER
  (GRAPHSCR)
   (SETVAR "BLIPMODE" 0)(SETVAR "CMDECHO" 0)
   (SETQ D2 (/ (GETDIST "\nPLEASE ENTER THE CAM MINIMUM DIA. ") 2)
         R (GETDIST "\nPLEASE ENTER THE MAXIMUM RISE (+) or FALL (-) ")
         S1 (* (/ PI 180)(GETREAL "\nENTER THE PROFILE START ANGLE (DEG.) "))
         P0 (GETPOINT "\nPLEASE PICK THE CAM CENTRE POINT ")
   )
   (COMMAND "UCS" "O" P0)
(SETQ AR1 (* (/ PI 180)(GETREAL"\nENTER THE TOTAL DISPLACEMENT ANGLE (DEG) "))
         A (/ AR1 90) A1 (/ PI 90)
         X (* D2 (COS S1)) Y (* D2 (SIN S1)) P1 (LIST X Y)
         PTS NIL PTS (CONS P1 PTS)
   )
     (REPEAT 90                ; 90 VECTORS IN THE PROFILE
      (SETQ D1 (+ (- (/ R 2)(* (/ R 2)(COS A1))) D2)
            Q (+ A S1)
            X1 (* D1 (COS Q)) Y1 (* D1 (SIN Q)) P2 (LIST X1 Y1)
            PTS (CONS P2 PTS)
            P1 P2 A (+ A(/ AR1 90)) A1 (+ A1 (/ PI 90))
      )
   )
     (SETQ PTS (REVERSE PTS))
     (COMMAND "PLINE" (FOREACH P PTS (COMMAND P)))
     (SETVAR "CMDECHO" 1)(SETVAR "BLIPMODE" 1)
     (COMMAND "UCS" "P")
     (PRINC)
)
```

If the cam profile is descending, enter a negative value in response to the screen prompt. Use the ARC command to construct any 'dwell' periods. The program uses a PLINE to save time when downloading to manufacture (via the DXFLINK) and continues the good practice of having the doing part of the program outside the loop.

I have not included the subroutine for the conversion of degrees to radians within the SHMK.LSP program as I would like you to modify the macro to include subroutines once you have successfully tested the program.

Whilst 'in-line' knife-edge followers are the most simple to program, other followers such as 'roller' and 'oscillating' followers can also be programmed using AutoLISP to construct the disk cam profile giving uniform velocity, simple harmonic motion or uniform acceleration and retardation. The drawing shows the difference between a simple knife-edge and a roller follower, for identical specifications (see Figure 44).

Figure 44

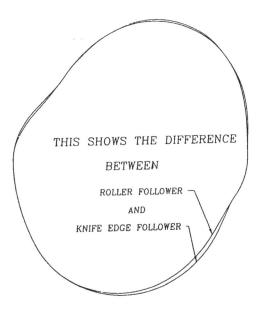

Stringing along

We need now to consider more string manipulation functions. In the recent past, lots of AutoLISP macros were designed to overcome the limitations of the AutoCAD TEXT command. Since those early days, more and more improvements with each new release has made most AutoLISP activities associated with string manipulation obsolete.

This being so there is still a good reason to be aware of the string manipulation functions and is necessary for those readers preparing for City & Guilds *AutoLISP Programming* certification (C&G 4351–005).

```
CH.LSP
(DEFUN C:CH ()                   ;Change Height (text)
 (SETQ A (SSGET))                ;Picks the text to be changed
 (SETQ HT (GETREAL "PLEASE ENTER THE TEXT HEIGHT "))
 (SETQ N (SSLENGTH A))           ;Number of entities to be changed
 (SETQ IN 0)                     ;Index=0 for first entity
  (REPEAT N                      ;"N" entities to be changed
   (SETQ NA (SSNAME A IN))       ;Select entity name to be changed
   (SETQ EL (ENTGET NA))         ;extract Entity List of NA
   (SETQ C (ASSOC 40 EL))        ;Extract a single element
                                 ;(Code 40 represents heigh)
   (SETQ B (CONS 40 HT))         ;CONstructs new list
   (SETQ D (SUBST B C EL))       ;SUBSTitute B for C in Entity List
   (ENTMOD D)                    ;ENTity MODification command
   (SETQ IN (1+ IN))             ;Increases the INdex by 1 in next loop
  )                              ;end of loop
(PRINC)
)
```

This program has only one new function:

■ **SUBST** – This substitutes one sublist for another and is often used in conjunction with the ASSOC function: '(SUBST <new list> <old list> <assoc list>)'. The ENTMOD function has to be used to change the drawing.

The program selects the line of text to be changed, extracts the height value from the first list (one list for each line of text) and substitutes this value with the new value in the first list prior to altering the database. At this point you will notice the change taking place on the screen. The above action is repeated in a loop for the second and remaining lists in the selected group of text.

At the command prompt enter:

```
!EL
```

Note the DXF code preceding the value that you entered for the text height 'HT'; look for the use of this code in the program CH.LSP.

When selecting the text you can use the 'window' or 'crossing' selection mode if you wish to edit the entire screen or part of the screen.

Problem 17

To create an AutoLISP macro that permits the editing of a string without the need to correct the entire line. Very often editing of text is required because of a simple spelling mistake, or the need to change a word and not the entire line. For early AutoCAD the inability to edit individual characters within a string was a real problem.

CHT.LSP

```
(DEFUN C:CHT () ;CHANGE TEXT
  (GRAPHSCR)
    (SETQ SS (CAR (ENTSEL "\nPICK THE TEXT TO BE CHANGED "))
          TC (GETSTRING "\nENTER THE WORD TO BE CHANGED ")
          SL (STRLEN TC)
          NT (GETSTRING "\nENTER THE NEW WORD ")
          SL2 (STRLEN NT)
          EG (ENTGET SS)
          TS (CDR (ASSOC 1 EG))
          TS2 (ASSOC 1 EG)
          SL3 (STRLEN TS) COUNT 1
    )
      (REPEAT SL3
        (SETQ OWORD (SUBSTR TS COUNT SL)
              CSL (+ COUNT SL) CSL2 (- SL3 CSL)
        )
        (IF (= OWORD TC)
            (PROGN (SETQ ST1 (SUBSTR TS 1 (1- COUNT)))
                   (SETQ ST2 (SUBSTR TS CSL (1+ CSL2)))
                   (SETQ NS (STRCAT ST1 NT ST2))
            )
        )
        (SETQ COUNT (1+ COUNT))
      )
      (SETQ SUBLST (CONS 1 NS)
            SUB (SUBST SUBLST TS2 EG))
      (ENTMOD SUB)
    (PRINC)
)
```

There are two new functions in this program:

- **STRLEN** – This function is used to determine the length or number of characters in a string.

```
(STRLEN "YES") returns 3
(STRLEN "YES" "NO") returns 5
(STRLEN " ") returns 0
(STRLEN "THIS IS A TEST") returns 14
```

- **SUBSTR** – This function removes a portion of a string; to start at a given point (counted in characters) and then remove a given number of characters:

```
(SETQ STRING "AutoLISP in Action")
(SUBSTR STRING 5 4) returns LISP
(SUBSTR STRING 13 3) returns Act
```

The program works by noting the length of the word to be changed and then extracting the actual line of text, looping through this line of text by increasing the start point one character at a time. Once the stated point is reached in the string that matches the word to be changed, the characters before and after this point are known and the string is re-built using the new word in place of the old.

Comments in the program are deliberately omitted because the best way to learn how the program works is to load and run it! If the test is successful, then enter the variables at the keyboard one at a time and note their values:

```
!SS
!TC
!SL
!NT
```

Continue until the end of the program; now add comments to CHT.LSP to describe each activity.

There is one more string manipulation function to cover:

- **STRCASE** – This function returns a string converted to upper or lower case (depending on the mode defined). If there is no mode defined then an upper-case string is returned.

```
(STRCASE "SAMPLE") returns "SAMPLE"
(STRCASE "SAMPLE" NIL) returns "SAMPLE"
(STRCASE "SAMPLE" T) returns "sample"
```

Problem 18
Break out

A directory devoted entirely to the symbols relating to your type of business is common place. This has not always been the case. One of the earliest requests for an AutoLISP macro involved the use of symbols inserted in the drawing from a standard library of symbols associated with some form of circuit design (such as electrical, hydraulic and pneumatic) or even flow diagrams. In each case the problem was the removal of that part of the circuit or diagram taken up by the inserted symbol. BOUT.LSP is an example program that solves this problem.

BOUT.LSP

```
(DEFUN C:BOUT () ; Break OUT
  (GRAPHSCR)
  (SETVAR "OSMODE" 512)(SETVAR "ATTDIA" 0)
   (SETQ COUNT 1 P1 T)
   (WHILE P1
    (SETQ P1 (GETPOINT "\nPICK INSERTION POINT "))
    (SETQ A (GETANGLE P1 "\nPICK 2nd POINT of BREAK-OUT "))
          (INITGET 1 "Battery Resistor Led Capacit")
          (SETQ B (GETKWORD "\nPLEASE ENTER THE BLOCK NAME "))
          (INITGET 1)
          (SETQ ATT (GETSTRING "\nPLEASE ENTER COMPONENT CODE "))
          (COND
            ((= B "Battery")(SETQ GAP 35))
            ((= B "Resistor")(SETQ GAP 52.5))
            ((= B "Led")(SETQ GAP 25))
            ((= B "Capacit")(SETQ GAP 30))
          )
          (SETQ P2 (POLAR P1 A GAP)
                AD (* A (/ 180 PI)))
          (COMMAND "BREAK" P1 P2
                   "INSERT" B P1 "" "" AD COUNT ATT)
          (SETQ COUNT (1+ COUNT))
          (INITGET 1 "C E")
```

```
               (SETQ TEST (GETKWORD "\nENTER C TO CONTINUE E TO END "))
                   (IF (= TEST "E")(SETQ P1 NIL))
        )                  ;END WHILE
     (SETVAR "OSMODE" 0)
     (PRINC)
  )
```

- **GETKWORD** – This function, with the aid of INITGET, is used to restrict the type of user's input. The INITGET function appears in the line above the GETKWORD function and includes the code '1' to inhibit a null response by pressing the 'Enter' key. This is followed by the required word or words inside quotation marks. These words can be abbreviated by the user to a single letter with AutoLISP returning the entire word if the first letter is upper case and the remainder of the word is lower, such as: '(INITGET 1 "Yes No")'.

  (INITGET 1 "Young Old")
  (SETQ TEST (GETKWORD "Would you describe yourself as
  Young or Old")) *respond with an empty return*
  Now enter Y *or* O
  !TEST *note the result*

- **GETANGLE** – This function pauses for the user to input an angle and returns that angle in radians. The user input can be directly from the keyboard (in degrees) or by picking (or using) two points:

  (SETQ TEST (GETANGLE "ENTER DEGREES"))
  Enter 45
  !TEST *returns* 0.7854 *(45 degrees in radians)*
  (SETQ TEST (GETANGLE "ENTER DEGREES"))
  Enter 180
  !TEST *returns* 3.1415 *('π' radians)*

Whilst dealing with GETANGLE we may as well cover the last of the required user input functions:

- **GETORIENT** – This function is similar to the GETANGLE function, except that the value of the angle returned by GETORIENT is unaffected by the system variables 'ANGBASE' and 'ANGDIR'. It always calculates the angle from the three o'clock position, in an anticlockwise direction (like the path of the sun rising from the East and setting in the West).

Whilst it is possible to alter the above variables with the UNITS command, I am afraid that if you do so all those AutoLISP macros involving trigonometrical functions will no longer behave in the expected manner. Leave well alone!

Before you can use the AutoLISP macro BOUT.LSP, it is necessary to draw the symbols as shown in Figure 45. The actual sizes are not all that important but the overall length of the symbols need to be as shown in the drawing as it is this length that we wish to remove from the line diagram.

Figure 45

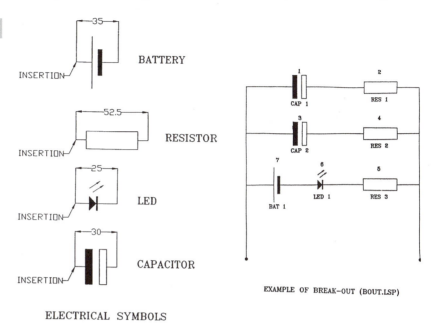

ELECTRICAL SYMBOLS
(USING THE WBLOCK COMMAND)

EXAMPLE OF BREAK-OUT (BOUT.LSP)

Create a WBLOCK of each symbol using the same name as shown (except 'CAPACITOR' which should be shortened to 'CAPACIT') and include two visible attributes, having no prompts or default values. The required attribute tags are 'code' and 'number'.

Make a line diagram (using angles to test the program). Load and run the program. Notice how the angle of each line is calculated from the two pick-points, and the length of gap in the line is determined from the multiple IF function COND. If there were only two possible test conditions then the IF function could have been used. In order to assist with the pick mode the OSNAP mode is set to 512 ('to the nearest line'). The 'ATTDIA' variable is also turned off so that the attribute dialog box does not appear, as this would present problems when using AutoLISP variables for the attribute values.

Parametrics

AutoLISP macros are particularly useful for what is often described as 'parametric' design. We have been dealing with parametrics since one of our first ever exercises (CONE.LSP), when the parameters were the height of the cone and the diameter of the cone.

All inserts are in a sense parametric because it is possible to vary the graphics scale along the 'X' axis independently of the 'Y' axis. For this to be of any value it is necessary for all the entities in a particular axis to be directly proportional to one another. This is not always the case, for example an 'I'-section beam can vary in breadth and/or depth without the fillet or thickness value changing, which leads me to the next problem involving the use of beams.

Problem 19
Purlin design

The next problem, and its program, has been chosen to:

- Introduce new functions.
- Satisfy the need of a local company.
- Simplify data reading.

In Problem 14 we began to link our AutoLISP macros with external files. we shall now re-visit this subject as it will help to solve the above problem.

File linking

Consider the integration of manufacturing and management data with the drawing file. The most obvious links include DXF files for manufacturing details and extracted text files for attribute details.

In the case of 'parametrics' there is a case for automatically creating a file that stores variable names with their current values resulting from the parametric program. Alternately, the parametric program could collect variable values directly from an external file. It is therefore necessary to be able to write to or read from an external file.

Writing

The program BEAM.LSP draws a simple sheet metal beam (see Figure 46). Incorporated within the program, however, is a material cutting list placed in an external file having the same name as the drawing but with the extension 'MAT'.

I have made use of the input value for the beam length to create a 3D drawing (you may not wish to do this).

BEAM.LSP

```
(DEFUN C:BEAM ()
(GRAPHSCR)
 (SETQ B (GETDIST "\nPLEASE ENTER THE BREADTH B: ")
       D (GETDIST "\nPLEASE ENTER THE DEPTH D: ")
```

➡

```
      T (GETDIST "\nPLEASE ENTER THE THICKNESS T: ")
       LE (GETDIST "\nPLEASE ENTER THE BEAM LENGTH ")
      M (GETSTRING T "\nPLEASE ENTER THE MATERIAL ")
     SM (STRCAT "MATERIAL= " M)
     W (+(-(* 2 B)T)(- D T))
    P1 (GETPOINT "\nPLEASE PICK THE INSERT POINT ")
)
(COMMAND "UCS" "O" P1)
  (COMMAND "THICKNESS" LE)
(SETQ P1 (LIST 0 0) P2 (LIST 0 (/ (- D) 2))
      P3 (POLAR P2 PI B) P4 (POLAR P3 (/ PI 2) T)
      P5 (LIST 0 (/ D 2)) P6 (POLAR P5 PI B)
      P7 (POLAR P6 (* (/ PI 2) 3) T)
)
  (SETQ DNAME (GETVAR "DWGNAME")
        MFILE (STRCAT DNAME ".MAT")) ;Material FILE
  (SETQ SW (STRCAT "CUTTING SIZE= " (RTOS W 2 2) " * ")
        SW2 (STRCAT SW (RTOS LE 2 2)))
  (SETQ OFILE (OPEN MFILE "w")) ;lower case,-OpenFILE
             (WRITE-LINE "MATERIAL CUTTING LIST" OFILE)
             (WRITE-LINE SM OFILE)
             (WRITE-LINE SW2 OFILE)
             (CLOSE OFILE)
(COMMAND "PLINE" P3 "W" "0" "0" P2 P5 P6 ""
         "FILLET" "R" (* 2 T) "FILLET" "P" P1
         "OFFSET" T P1 P4 ""
         "LINE" P3 P4 "" "LINE" P6 P7 ""
         "UCS" "P"
)
)
```

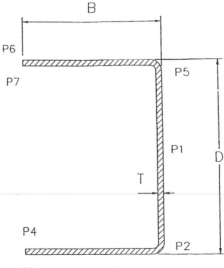

Figure 46

Open a drawing making a note of the drawing name. Load and run the macro. At the command prompt enter:

TYPE [*your drawing name*].MAT *(Ref.: ACAD.PGP file)*

This should reveal the material cutting list which can then be made available to the production department for use during any further processing.

Reading

Parametric programs can collect data by reading an external file such as a database or spreadsheet. If there are a number of fixed or limited parameters then an easy solution, and one that I prefer to use, is to store the data in a simple ASCII file, one line at a time.

When different variables in a parametric program are not directly proportional, and are entered at the keyboard one at a time (like the standard 'I'-section beam), there is always the possibility of a mistake. It is also time consuming, especially if the data has to be collected from separate sources such as tables, catalogues and manuals.

For such problems it would be ideal to store the necessary data in such a way as to be directly accessible by an AutoLISP program. There is no need to resort to complex database packages, take the simple option and create the necessary data file as an ASCII file.

I have deliberately simplified this first attempt. In practice, the number of variables and entities in the database would be much larger.

I have chosen six different 'ward purlins' for the example and limited the database variables to height ('HT'), width ('WI') and thickness ('TH') – see Figure 47.

Figure 47

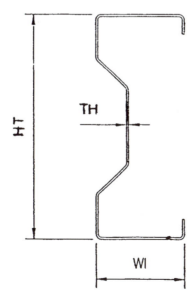

The different variables are to be stored in an external database and used by the AutoLISP macro to calculate the remaining geometry prior to completing the drawing.

I will develop the program in stages, starting with the database.

Create the following ASCII file (name it 'PURLIN.DAT' and, for simplicity, place the file in your working directory:

```
;  blank line
**1
120,56,1.50
**2
140,70,1.55
**3
170,70,1.60
**4
200,70,1.60
**5
230,70,1.80
**6
260,70,2.00
```

Remember to leave a blank line at the top of the file. Use comma-delimited format (CDF) or space-delimited format (SDF) for your data file, but make sure that your AutoLISP file is consistent. I have used CDF as you can see; do not place a comma after the last entity in each line of data.

Figure 48

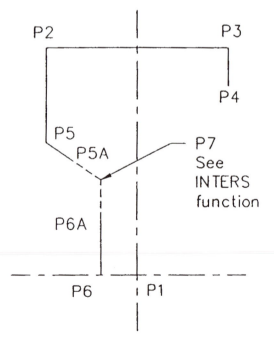

The two asterisks ('**') are used in conjunction with an integer to create a unique tag to locate a particular record of data. You can use any tag you like, but remember that this tag must appear once only in the file and must not form part of a record.

You do not have to use the same tag as I have done, but your tag must be consistent with the AutoLISP macro.

Now let us develop the macro in stages.

PURLIN.LSP

```
(DEFUN C:PURLIN ()
(GRAPHSCR)
(SETQ CODE (GETINT "\nPLEASE ENTER THE REQUIRED CODE NUMBER "))
(SETQ NUMBER (STRCAT "**" (ITOA CODE)))
(SETQ PD (OPEN "PURLIN.DAT" "r"))
(SETQ FIND (READ-LINE PD)) ; Blank line
  (WHILE FIND ; Find data relative to code No.
    (SETQ FIND (READ-LINE PD))
    (IF (= FIND NUMBER)
                    (SETQ DATA (READ-LINE PD) FIND NIL)
    )
  )
  (CLOSE PD)
)
```

Load and run PURLIN.LSP, responding to the prompt with a number between one and six. At the command line enter:

```
!DATA
```

You should have extracted the required data from the database. Unfortunately, the data is in the form of a string and any further usage in this format is limited.

Parsing

The next stage is to convert the string into a LIST containing three entities which can, at a later stage, be allocated to the variables 'HT', 'WI' and 'TH'.

PURLIN2.LSP

```
(DEFUN C:PURLIN2 ()
(GRAPHSCR)
(SETQ CODE (GETINT "\nPLEASE ENTER THE REQUIRED CODE NUMBER "))
(SETQ NUMBER (STRCAT "**" (ITOA CODE)))
(SETQ PD (OPEN "PURLIN.DAT" "r"))
(SETQ FIND (READ-LINE PD)) ; Blank line
```
➡

```
  (WHILE FIND                    ; Find data relative to code No.
   (SETQ FIND (READ-LINE PD))
   (IF (= FIND NUMBER)
                     (SETQ DATA (READ-LINE PD) FIND NIL)
   )
  )
 (IF DATA
  (PROGN
      (SETQ SLENGTH (STRLEN DATA) ; Length of string
            COUNT 1 CHAR 1)
      (WHILE (< COUNT SLENGTH)
       (IF (/= "," (SUBSTR DATA COUNT 1))
           (SETQ CHAR (1+ CHAR)) ; If not "," increment in loop
           (SETQ NUM (ATOF (SUBSTR DATA (1+ (- COUNT CHAR)) CHAR))
               DATALST (APPEND DATALST (LIST NUM)) CHAR 1)
       )
       (SETQ COUNT (1+ COUNT)) ; Increment counter
      )
      (SETQ NUM (ATOF (SUBSTR DATA (1+ (- COUNT CHAR)))))
            DATALST (APPEND DATALST (LIST NUM)))
  )
 )
 (CLOSE PD)
)
```

You do not have to rename PURLIN.LSP. I have given each stage a new name for clarity.

In order to extract part of the string we use the STRLEN function to find its length and the SUBSTR function to extract the data separated by the commas. The number of characters in each individual string is counted within the loop, searching for the comma. Finally, the individual strings are returned as real numbers, by using the new function ATOF. (Note the use of '/=' not equal expression). The LIST is completed by the new function APPEND.

■ **ATOF** – Converts a string to a floating point number:

```
(ATOF "1.23") returns 1.23
(ATOF "2") returns 2.0
(ATOF "2.31xx36") returns 2.31
(SETQ TEST "1.23)
(TYPE TEST) returns STR
(SETQ TEST(ATOF "1.23"))
(TYPE TEST) returns REAL
```

■ **APPEND** – This function generates a list by appending several lists together. The new list will be a single list in the same order as that used by the function.

```
(APPEND '(1 2) '(3 4) '(5 6) returns (1 2 3 4 5 6)
(SETQ A(LIST 1 2))
(SETQ B(LIST 3 4))
(APPEND A B) returns (1 2 3 4)
```

Load and run PURLIN2.LSP. Then, at the command prompt, enter:

```
!DATALIST  note the result
(TYPE DATA)  note the result
(TYPE DATALST)  also noting the resultant string and real entity
```

We need now to allocate variable names to the different entities or values within the list by using a new function:

■ **MAPCAR** – This function returns, as a list, the result of executing a particular function on the individual values in a list. This seems a little complicated to me. Let us simplify things with practical examples before completing the PURLIN macro:

```
(SETQ A 5 B 8 C 10)
(MAPCAR '1+ (LIST A B C )) returns (6 9 11)
(MAPCAR '+ '(10 12 14) '(5 7 3)) returns (15 19 17)
```

See Figure 49 and 3DL.LSP below, a simple line problem in 3D to demonstrate the MAPCAR function.

3D.LSP

```
(DEFUN 3DL (P1 P2)
 (SETQ DIST (MAPCAR '- P2 P1)
       SQPT (MAPCAR '* DIST DIST)
       SUM (APPLY '+ SQPT)
       3DLEN (SQRT SUM) ;LENGTH of "3D" LINE
 )
)
```

Figure 49

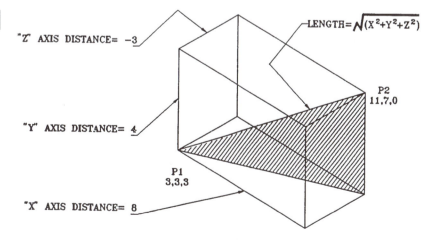

"Z" AXIS DISTANCE= −3

$LENGTH = \sqrt{(X^2 + Y^2 + Z^2)}$

P2
11,7,0

"Y" AXIS DISTANCE= 4

P1
3,3,3

"X" AXIS DISTANCE= 8

At the comand prompt, try:

```
(SETQ P1 (LIST 3 3 3))
(SETQ P2 (LIST 11 7 0))
LINE
FROM POINT: type !P1
TO POINT: type !P2
```

The program determines the distance between two points in space having different coordinate values. Load and run 3DL.LSP by entering:

```
(3DL P1 P2)
```

The program returns 9.43398 (the last value of the variable '3DLEN'). Now enter:

```
LIST
```

Select the LINE and note the value for the 3D length.

The mathematics involved in the program is quite easy to work out for those familiar with Pythagoras' Theorem.

Note the use of 'arguments' 'P1' and 'P2', passed to the program from outside (See 'Passing an argument, *AutoLISP in Action*, page 24).

I have deliberately used integer values for 'x', 'y' and 'z' to help simplify the mathematics. The best way of understanding the MAPCAR function is to enter the following:

```
!DIST
```

This calculates the distances 'x', 'y' and 'z' (see Figure 49).

```
!SQRT
```

This creates a list of the squares of 'x', 'y' and 'z' (that is, to the power two).

```
!SUM
```

The sum of all the squares in the list.

```
!3DLEN
```

This results in the length of the line, or the distance between the two points (equal to $\sqrt{x^2 + y^2 + z^2}$).

Now back to PURLIN3.LSP. you should now be able to work out the value of the following function:

```
(MAPCAR 'SET ' (HT WI TH) DATALST)
```

Enter '!DATALST' if you have forgotten its contents.

The revised macro (PURLIN3.LSP) completes the graphics on the screen, but information relating to the code number for each different purlin is necessary for the successful use of the program.

PURLIN3.LSP

```
(DEFUN C:PURLIN3 ()
(GRAPHSCR)
(SETQ CODE (GETINT "\nPLEASE ENTER THE REQUIRED CODE NUMBER "))
(SETQ NUMBER (STRCAT "**" (ITOA CODE)))
(SETQ PD (OPEN "PURLIN.DAT" "r"))
(SETQ FIND (READ-LINE PD)) ; Blank line
  (WHILE FIND                ; Find data relative to code No.
    (SETQ FIND (READ-LINE PD))
    (IF (= FIND NUMBER)
                       (SETQ DATA (READ-LINE PD) FIND NIL)
    )
  )
 (IF DATA
  (PROGN
      (SETQ SLENGTH (STRLEN DATA) ; Length of string
            COUNT 1 CHAR 1)
      (WHILE (< COUNT SLENGTH)
        (IF (/= "," (SUBSTR DATA COUNT 1))
            (SETQ CHAR (1+ CHAR)) ; If not "," increment in loop
            (SETQ NUM (ATOF (SUBSTR DATA (1+ (- COUNT CHAR)) CHAR))
                  DATALST (APPEND DATALST (LIST NUM)) CHAR 1)
        )
        (SETQ COUNT (1+ COUNT)) ; Increment counter
       )
     (SETQ NUM (ATOF (SUBSTR DATA (1+ (- COUNT CHAR))))
           DATALST (APPEND DATALST (LIST NUM)))
 )
)
(CLOSE PD)
(MAPCAR 'SET '(HT WI TH) DATALST)
(SETQ P1 (GETPOINT "\nPLEASE PICK THE PURLIN CENTRE POINT "))
(COMMAND "UCS" "O" P1)
(SETQ P1 (LIST 0 0) P3 (LIST (/ WI 2)(/ HT 2))
      P2 (POLAR P3 PI WI) P4 (POLAR P3 (* (/ PI 2) 3) 15)
      P5 (POLAR P2 (* (/ PI 2) 3) 34)
      P6 (POLAR P1 PI (- (/ WI 2) 25))
      P5A (POLAR P5 (- 0 0.7217) 5)
      P6A (POLAR P6 (/ PI 2) 5)
      P7 (INTERS P5 P5A P6 P6A NIL)
      P8 (POLAR P1 PI (/ WI 2)))
(COMMAND "PLINE" P6 "W" 0 0 P7 P5 P2 P3 P4 ""
         "FILLET" "R" 4 ""
         "FILLET" "P" P3 "OFFSET" TH P6 P1 ""
         "LINE" P4 (POLAR P4 PI TH) ""
         "MIRROR" "W" P8 P3 "" P8 P1 "" "UCS" "P")
  (SETQ DATALST NIL)          ; Prepare for new list
)
```

Using your purlin macro, create a slide file (MSLIDE) as shown in the Figure 50 and add the VSLIDE command to PURLIN3.LSP.

Figure 50

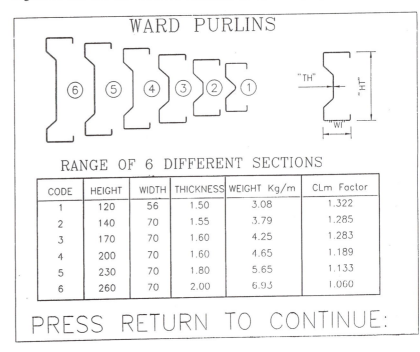

I think the VSLIDE command is most satisfactory for this type of problem, although there are those who prefer pull-down screen icons. One addition you should make to the program would be to control the input values. The final macro is shown in PURLIN4.LSP

PURLIN4.LSP

```
(DEFUN C:PURLIN4 ()
(GRAPHSCR)
(COMMAND "VSLIDE" "PURLIN" PAUSE "REDRAW")
(SETQ CODE (GETINT "\nPLEASE ENTER THE REQUIRED CODE NUMBER "))
(SETQ NUMBER (STRCAT "**" (ITOA CODE)))
(SETQ PD (OPEN "PURLIN.DAT" "r"))
(SETQ FIND (READ-LINE PD))   ; Blank line
  (WHILE FIND                ; Find data relative to code No.
    (SETQ FIND (READ-LINE PD))
    (IF (= FIND NUMBER)
                (SETQ DATA (READ-LINE PD) FIND NIL)
    )
  )
(IF DATA
  (PROGN
      (SETQ SLENGTH (STRLEN DATA) ; Length of string
          COUNT 1 CHAR 1)
```

```
      (WHILE (< COUNT SLENGTH)
       (IF (/= "," (SUBSTR DATA COUNT 1))
            (SETQ CHAR (1+ CHAR)) ; If not "," increment in loop
             (SETQ NUM (ATOF (SUBSTR DATA (1+ (- COUNT CHAR)) CHAR))
                 DATALST (APPEND DATALST (LIST NUM)) CHAR 1)
        )
        (SETQ COUNT (1+ COUNT)) ; Increment counter
       )
      (SETQ NUM (ATOF (SUBSTR DATA (1+ (- COUNT CHAR))))
            DATALST (APPEND DATALST (LIST NUM)))
  )
)
(CLOSE PD)
(MAPCAR 'SET '(HT WI TH) DATALST)
(SETQ P1 (GETPOINT "\nPLEASE PICK THE PURLIN CENTRE POINT "))
(COMMAND "UCS" "O" P1)
(SETQ P1 (LIST 0 0) P3 (LIST (/ WI 2)(/ HT 2))
      P2 (POLAR P3 PI WI) P4 (POLAR P3 (* (/ PI 2) 3) 15)
      P5 (POLAR P2 (* (/ PI 2) 3) 34)
      P6 (POLAR P1 PI (- (/ WI 2) 25))
      P5A (POLAR P5 (- 0 0.7217) 5)
      P6A (POLAR P6 (/ PI 2) 5)
      P7 (INTERS P5 P5A P6 P6A NIL)
      P8 (POLAR P1 PI (/ WI 2)))
(COMMAND "PLINE" P6 "W" 0 0 P7 P5 P2 P3 P4 ""
         "FILLET" "R" 4 ""
         "FILLET" "P" P3 "OFFSET" TH P6 P1 ""
         "LINE" P4 (POLAR P4 PI TH) ""
         "MIRROR" "W" P8 P3 "" P8 P1 "" "UCS" "P")
  (SETQ DATALST NIL) ; Prepare for new list
)
```

Try to make all your programmes "idiot proof", it has been a hard lesson that I have had to learn.

In 3DL.LSP, we used a new function:

▪ **APPLY** – This function passes an argument in the list:

```
(SETQ LIST '(1 6 2 88))
(APPLY '* LIST) Returns 768
```

APPLY processes the list as a whole, in contrast to MAPCAR, which processes individual elements of a list; it has the same effect as CONS and EVAL:

▪ **EVAL** – This function evaluates an expression. Remember the contents of our list (1 6 2 8 8); try:

```
(EVAL (CONS '* LIST))
```

This returns the same as above for the APPLY function i.e. 768.

Problem 20

Architectural drawings can contain a large number of standard parts *inserted* within them. The request was for an AutoLISP program that would determine the number of times each item of stock was used in each contract, for instance how many three-point electric sockets are there in a specific building? (Who wants to count them on the drawing?)

The only new function in the next program is:

■ **AND** – If any of the expressions in the list '(AND ...)' evaluates to NIL, this function ceases further evaluation:

```
COMMAND: (SETQ A 103 B NIL C "STRING")
(AND 1.4 A C) Returns T
(AND 1.4 A B C) Returns NIL
```

The function is also very useful when you wish to check the condition of two or more expressions. There must obviously be a minimum of two expressions in the test condition. At the command prompt try:

```
LINE
FROM POINT: 50,50
TO POINT: 100,75
(SETQ TEST 15)
(IF (AND (> TEST 10) (< TEST 20)
        (COMMAND "ERASE" "L" "")))
```

This can be read as: *If* test is less than 20 *and* more than 10 *then* erase the last item ('L' for 'last').

In INSERTQ.LSP the test condition checks to see *if* the variable equals 'INSERT' *and* the selected name is equal to the input name *then* the count is incremented by one.

INSERTQ.LSP

```
(DEFUN C:INSERTQ () ; INSERT Quantities
  (SETQ COUNT 0)
  (SETQ NAME (STRCASE (GETSTRING "\nPLEASE ENTER THE INSERT NAME ")))
  (SETQ EN (ENTNEXT))
```
➧

```
←
   (WHILE (SETQ EN (ENTNEXT EN))
     (SETQ BLK (CDR (ASSOC 0 (ENTGET EN)))) ; BLocK
     (SETQ BLN (CDR (ASSOC 2 (ENTGET EN)))) ; BLock Name
(IF (AND (EQ BLK "INSERT")(EQ BLN NAME))(SETQ COUNT (1+ COUNT)))
   )
  (PROMPT (STRCAT "THE NUMBER OF "NAME " INSERTS= "(ITOA NUM )))
(PRINC)
)
```

Load and run the program on an existing drawing containing multiple inserts of blocks. I tested the program on Figure 51 (this is a figure supplied with AutoCAD by Autodesk – C:\ACAD\DWGS\SITE-3D.DWG).

Figure 51

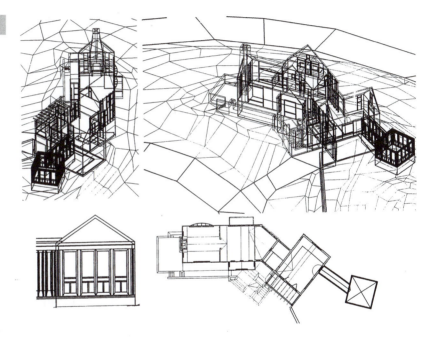

Run the program to determine how many times the block 'CUBE' has been inserted in the drawing – I found 43. The program prompts the user for the name of the required insert and then searches the drawing database, counting the number of times (with the COUNT function) it encounters the insert name. This value is then displayed in the prompt area of the screen.

Whilst on the subject of logical operators we may as well cover the remaining two functions: NOT and OR.

■ **NOT** – This function returns 'T' if the item evaluated equals NIL:

```
(SETQ A 123 B "STRING" C NIL)
(NOT A) Returns NIL
(NOT C) Returns T
```

When reading a line in an external file such as '(SETQ READL (READLINE FILE))' we often use this in a loop that terminates '(WHILE READL ...)' once the end of the file is reached. We could use the NOT function to detect this condition and to close the file with:

```
(IF (NOT READL) (CLOSE FILE))
```

That is: *If* 'READL' equals NIL *then* close the file.

■ **OR** – This function (unlike the AND function that requires all expressions to be true) requires only one expression to be true:

```
(OR NIL 45 '( ))  Returns T
```

Once a non-NIL expression is encountered the function ceases further evaluation and returns true. For instance, at the command prompt:

```
LINE
FROM POINT: 50,50
TO POINT: 100,75
(SETQ TEST (GETSTRING ⏎
        "DO YOU WISH TO ERASE THE LINE Y/N?"))
(IF(OR(= TEST "Y") (= TEST "y"))⏎
        (COMMAND "ERASE" "L" ""))
(SETQ A 26 B 10)
(IF(OR (< A B) (> A 25)) (SETQ C 5))
```

If 'A' is less than 'B' *or* 'A' is greater than 25 *then* set 'C' to 5 *else* do nothing. Now enter:

```
!C
```

And note the result.

List extraction functions

We have already covered ASSOC, CAR, CDR, CADR and CADDR functions, which leaves us with just two more to understand, NTH and LAST.

■ **NTH** – This function enables you to extract any item you wish from a list, and is extremely useful. All that is needed is the knowledge of the position in the list of the required item.

In *AutoLISP in Action*, one of our first programs was REC.LSP, a simple program for drawing a rectangle from two 'pick-points'.

Load and run REC.LSP followed by:

```
!P1
(SETQ A(CAR P1))   Note the value
(SETQ B(CADR P1))  Note the value
```

Now test the NTH function; enter:

```
(SETQ C (NTH 0 P1))
```

This should be the same value as variable 'A' above; note that the count for the NTH function starts at zero and not at one. Now enter:

```
(SETQ D(NTH 1 P1)) Note the result
(SETQ E(NTH 2 P1))
```

This should confirm the function; if the number exceeds the length of the list, then NIL is returned.

```
(SETQ F(NTH 3 P1)) 'P1' is of course a list, and should return NIL
!P2 Repeat the above if you need convincing
```

■ **LAST** – This is the last of the list extraction functions and simply returns the last element in a list, be it an atom, or a list within a list:

```
(LAST '(A B C D E)) Returns E
(LAST '(A B C (D E))) Returns (D E)
(SETQ P1 '(1.2 3.4 5.6))
(LAST P1) Returns 5.6
```

The list 'P1' could represent the 'x', 'y' and 'z' values for a point in space, you could also extract these values by using (CAR (X)), (CADR (Y)) and CADDR to obtain the 'z' value:

```
(CADDR P1)
```

Returns the same value as '(LAST P1)'. I prefer to use the LAST function to extract the last entity from lists which are greater than three entities long.

Printing to the screen

There are four similar functions for printing to the screen. We have already covered PRINC and PROMPT which are the most common AutoLISP functions which display a string in the command prompt area. The remaining two functions are PRIN1 and PRINT.

■ **PRIN1** – Very similar to the PRINC function but displays any control characters such as '\n' without acting upon them. It can also be used to print to a file and in conjunction with the function CHR. At the command prompt:

```
(SETQ TEST 59)
(PRIN1 A) Prints 59 and returns 59
(PRIN1 "GREAT") Prints GREAT and returns GREAT but...
(PRIN1 "GREAT" FILE) Also writes GREAT to the file called FILE
(PRIN1 (CHR 37)) Prints % and returns %
(PRIN1 (CHR 92)) Prints \ and returns \
```

■ CHR – This function returns the actual letter or graphics character equivalent to the ASCII number given in the form of a string (see Figure 52). At the command prompt:

```
(ASCII "T") Returns 84
(ASCII "$") Returns 36
```

Make sure that the letters or characters are enclosed with quotes.

Figure 52

ASCII code	Character	ASCII code	Character	ASCII code	Character
32	blank space	64	@	96	'
33	!	65	A	97	a
34	"	66	B	98	b
35	#	67	C	99	c
36	$	68	D	100	d
37	%	69	E	101	e
38	&	70	F	102	f
39	'	71	G	103	g
40	(	72	H	104	h
41	)	73	I	105	i
42	*	74	J	106	j
43	+	75	K	107	k
44	'	76	L	108	l
45	–	77	M	109	m
46	.	78	N	110	n
47	/	79	O	111	o
48	0	80	P	112	p
49	1	81	Q	113	q
50	2	82	R	114	r
51	3	83	S	115	s
52	4	84	T	116	t
53	5	85	U	117	u
54	6	86	V	118	v
55	7	87	W	119	w
56	8	88	X	120	x
57	9	89	Y	121	y
58	:	90	Z	122	z
59	;	91	[	123	{
60	<	92	\	124		
61	=	93	]	125	}
62	>	94	^	126	~
63	?	95	_		

To see the simplified range of ASCII codes enter and run ASCTXT.LSP.

ASCTXT.LSP

```
(DEFUN c:ASCTXT ()
 (TEXTSCR)
 (SETQ COUNT 33)
  (REPEAT 222
    (PRINT COUNT)( PRINC "=")(PRIN1 (CHR COUNT))
    (PRINC "\t") ;TAB BETWEEN PRINT
    (SETQ COUNT (1+ COUNT))
  )
 (PRINC)
)
```

▓ **PRINT** – This function can be used to write to a file in the same way as PRINC and PRIN1. When PRINT is used to write a string to a file it starts a new line and attaches one blank space after the string (note the results from ASCTXT.LSP).

In general use PRINC or PROMPT for all your routine message displays. When PRINC is used it removes the quotation marks but does not start a new line, this is why we use the '\n' control code in conjunction with PRINC to start the message on a new line. Remember that PRIN1 does not start the string on a new line and does not respond to control codes such as '\n'.

Forging ahead

You should now have sufficient confidence with AutoLISP to hammer out a few ornamental wrought-iron problems. In recent years, ecclesiastical wrought ironwork has regained some of its previous popularity and it is hoped that the severity of some of our modern buildings may be relieved by the more traditional form of decoration.

These designs are based on a series of 'S' and 'C' scrolls in proportions that give beauty and grace to gates, grilles, screens, etc. (See SCROLL.LSP and Figure 53.)

SCROLL.LSP

```
(DEFUN C:SCROLL ()
 (GRAPHSCR)
 (SETVAR "CMDECHO" 0)(SETVAR "BLIPMODE" 0)
  (SETQ P1 (GETPOINT "\nPLEASE PICK THE CENTRE OF SCROLL "))
  (COMMAND "UCS" "O" P1)
  (SETQ R 1 P1 (LIST R 0) RATIO 1.02
        PTS NIL PTS (CONS P1 PTS)
        A (/ PI 45))
  (PROMPT "\nNEGATIVE CLOCKWISE: POSITIVE ANTICLOCKWISE: ")
```
➡

```
(SETQ ANG (/ (GETDIST "\nENTER THE SCROLL ANGLE (DEG.) ")(/ 180 PI)))
   (IF (< ANG 0)(SETQ A (- A)))
    (SETQ B A NA (/ ANG (/ PI 45))
          N (FIX NA) N (ABS N))
    (REPEAT N
    (SETQ MR (* R RATIO)
          X (* MR (COS A)) Y (* MR (SIN A))
          P2 (LIST X Y)
          PTS (CONS P2 PTS)
          P1 P2 A (+ A B) R MR
     )
    )
    (SETQ PTS (REVERSE PTS))
    (COMMAND "PLINE" (FOREACH P PTS (COMMAND P)))
    (SETVAR "CMDECHO" 1)(SETVAR "BLIPMODE" 1)
    (COMMAND "UCS" "P")
    (PRINC)
)
```

Figure 53

The scroll variables can be altered to give a series of shapes that can be inserted, copied, scaled, arrayed, and mirrored to complete the design.

The program expects any PLINE width to be set prior to using the macro. The program allows you to select the start point (centre of scroll) and to input the scroll rotation angle of your choice, clockwise or anticlockwise. I found 1.02 a suitable value for the scroll ratio 'RAT' (alter this value to suit your own needs). The vectors used to construct the scroll are drawn every four degrees (π/45 radians), this too can be altered to suit. There is only one new function included in this program:

■ **ABS** – This function is used to return a positive value for 'N' when the input value for 'ANG' is negative. At the command prompt:

```
(ABS  59)      Returns  59
(ABS  -60)     Returns  60
(ABS  -60.25)  Returns  60.25
```

Problem 21
This could be 'sad'

For our next problem, let's look a little closer into the AutoCAD database and use two new AutoLISP functions:

- **SSADD** – This function is often used with an entity name and a selection set: '(SSADD <entity name> <selection set>)'. It *adds* the named entity to the selection set.
- **SSDEL** – This function *deletes* the entity name from the selection set: '(SSDEL <entity name> <selection set>). The entity is physically deleted from the selection set as opposed to a new string being returned with the element deleted.

Figure 54

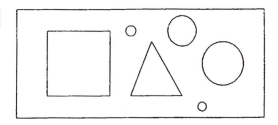

The new functions involve the addition and subtraction of entities from a particular selection set and is best illustrated by the following exercise:

1. Create a drawing similar to the one shown, using the PLINE and CIRCLE commands.
2. At the command prompt enter the following:

```
(SETQ SS1 (SSGET))  Window the entire drawing selection
(SSLENGTH SS1)  Note the value
(SSDEL (SETQ OUTLINE (CAR (ENTSEL))) SS1)
Pick the outline on the drawing
SELECT
!SS1  Note the effect of  SSDEL
(SSADD OUTLINE SS1)
SELECT
!SS1  Note the effect of  SSADD
```

Predicate test functions

We are supposed to be able to use and describe seven different predicate functions. I have got to admit that the three most commonly used functions are the ones that we have already used: EQ, EQUAL and NULL; now for the remainder.

- **ATOM** – This function returns NIL if the item (ATOM <item>) is a list, and T otherwise; anything that is not a list is considered an ATOM.
- **LISTP** – This function returns T if the item (LISTP <item>) is a list, and NIL otherwise (this is the opposite of ATOM).
- **BOUNDP** – This function returns T if the atom (BOUNDP <atom>) has a value bound to it:

```
(SETQ A 2 B NIL)
(BOUNDP 'A) Returns T
(BOUNDP 'B) Returns NIL
```

- **NUMBERP** – This function returns T if the item (NUMBERP <item>) is real or an integer:

```
(SETQ A 123 B 'A)
(NUMBERP 4) Returns T
(NUMBERP 1.2345) Returns T
(NUMBERP "BOREDOM") Returns NIL
(NUMBERP A) Returns T
(NUMBERP B) Returns NIL
```

There are more predicate test functions but the need for more practical activities brings me to a recent problem associated with the leisure industry.

Problem 22
Round the bend and up the twist

A company who designs and manufactures modern sport and leisure sites associated with water were experiencing design limitations in terms of two-dimensional (2D) graphics and wished to express the more complex spiral water slides and risers in 3D for presentation as rendered images.

The solution had to be limited to AutoCAD without the EXTRUDE command. See SPIRAL.LSP and Figure 55.

SPIRAL.LSP

```
(DEFUN C:SPIRAL ()
(GRAPHSCR)
 (SETVAR "BLIPMODE" 0)(SETVAR "CMDECHO" 0)
 (SETQ P1 (GETPOINT "\nPLEASE PICK THE CENTRE OF SPIRAL "))
 (SETQ R (GETREAL "\nPLEASE ENTER THE SPIRAL RAD VALUE: "))
 (SETQ AS (GETREAL "\nPLEASE ENTER THE ANGLE FOR EACH STEP "))
 (SETQ H (GETREAL "\nPLEASE ENTER THE SPIRAL LEAD "))
 (SETQ ASR (/ AS (/ 180 PI)))
 (SETQ RAT (/ H 40)) ;spiral ratio
 (COMMAND "UCS" "O" P1)
 (SETQ P1 (LIST R 0 0))
 (SETQ A (/ PI 20) B A)
 (SETQ Q T Z RAT PTS NIL PTS (CONS P1 PTS))
  (WHILE Q
   (SETQ X (* R (COS A)))
   (SETQ Y (* R (SIN A)))
   (SETQ P2 (LIST X Y Z) PTS (CONS P2 PTS))
   (SETQ P3 (LIST 0 0 Z))
   (IF (>= B ASR)(PROGN
                     (COMMAND "LINE" P3 P2 "")
                     (SETQ B 0)
                 ))
   (SETQ P1 P2)
   (SETQ A (+ A (/ PI 20)))
   (SETQ B (+ B (/ PI 20)))
   (SETQ Z (+ Z RAT))
   (IF (> A (* 4 PI))(SETQ Q NIL))
  )
```

➡

```
(SETQ PTS (REVERSE PTS))
(COMMAND "3DPOLY" (FOREACH P PTS (COMMAND P)))
(COMMAND "LINE" P3 (LIST 0 0) "")
(COMMAND "UCS" "P")
(SETVAR "CMDECHO" 1)(SETVAR "BLIPMODE" 1)
(PRINC)
)
```

Figure 55

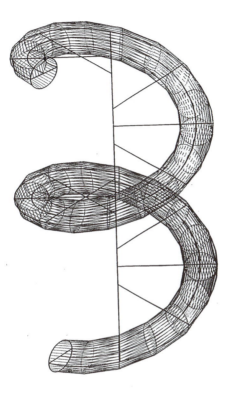

The AutoLISP macro prompts for the radius value ('RAD'); it is necessary to run the macro three times to give the central axis followed by the inner and outer radius values – all having the same spiral lead (my example shows a lead of $2 \times$ 'RAD').

The step angle (45° in this example) defines the radiating spokes that support the structure from a central pillar.

Once the three spirals have been constructed (the 3DPOLY AutoCAD command) move the UCS to the two ends of the central spiral to construct the two circles (broken at the intersection points with the inner and outer spiral), before using the EDGESURF command having previously set the SURFTAB1 and SURFTAB2 variables to suitable values. Remember that this is only a schematic drawing to show the principle involved.

More string conversion functions

In previous exercises we have used the RTOS function which converts a real number to a string.

- **ANGTOS** – This function converts angles to a string in a similar manner to RTOS. The function takes an angle (a real number in radians). For instance:

```
(ANGTOS <ANGLE> <MODE> <PRECISION> ...)
```

This returns it edited into a string in the format of the specified mode.

0   Degrees
1   Degrees/minutes/seconds
2   Grads
3   Radians
4   Surveyor's units

```
(ANGTOS PI 0 4 ) Returns 180.0000
(ANGTOS PI 3 2) Returns 3.14r ('r' for rounded)
(ANGTOS 0.785398 0 3) Returns 45.000
(ANGTOS -0.785398 0 1) Returns 315.0
```

The need for string conversion functions is often due to the need to read from or write to an external file. These files will have a string data-type. If, however, calculations are to be performed on such data, it is necessary to convert the string data to a real or integer value:

- **ITOA** – This function converts an integer to a string.

```
(ITOA 35) Returns 35
(ITOA -35) Returns -35
(SETQ TEST (ITOA 59)) Returns 59
!TEST Returns 59
(TYPE TEST) Returns STR
(SETQ TEST 59)
(TYPE TEST) Returns INT
```

- **ATOI** – This is the last string conversion function. It converts an integer into a string, i.e. the opposite of ITOA. It reads only to the first non-numeric character.

```
(ATOI "1") Returns 1
(ATOI "1.2345") Returns 1
```
The decimal point is a non-numeric character
```
(ATOI "1 2 3") Returns 1
```
The space is the first non-numeric character
```
(ATOI "123") Returns 123
```

Problem 23
A 3D adventure

In our last problem we helped to solve the visualisation of a rather complex 3D image. Increasingly, computer graphics are required in 3D at the design stage of the activity. This technology will grow rapidly in the next few years at the expense of 2D and hopefully all '2$\frac{1}{2}$D' (isometric) graphics.

I now wish to introduce you to the 3DMESH command to solve a problem involving a universal microscope (see Figure 56). This drawing was drawn in 2$\frac{1}{2}$D and is of little value other than an illustration, it does not lend itself to 3D visualisation, rendering or orthographic projection as the database consists of 2D points only (there are no 'z' values – the drawing is 'flat' even though it looks 3D).

Figure 56

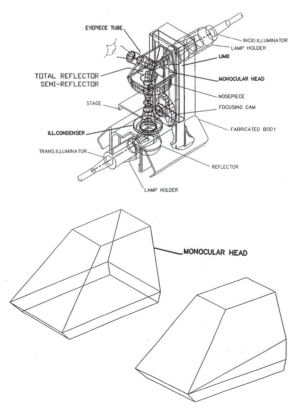

The drawing formed part of a design project for college and university students and required the design of a fool-proof universal microscope involving a series of manufacturing processes.

Our problem is to devise an AutoLISP macro in surface modelling to help with the monocular head design. The finished model must be transferable to rendering packages for improved visualisation. The design parameters are the lengths and angles.

It is possible to build up the design by a series of 3DFACE commands. However, a better solution would be to use the 3DMESH command for each different side of the rectangle. Using the 3DMESH command directly from the keyboard is not recommended because any editing (or correcting of errors) requires the re-input of every entity all over again.

The solution is to use a 'script' file, or as in our case, an AutoLISP program that calculates each point from the input parameters before using these points within the 3DMESH command. See MONO.LSP below.

MONO.LSP

```
(DEFUN C:MONO ()
 (GRAPHSCR)
 (SETVAR "CMDECHO" 0)
 (SETQ P1 (GETPOINT "\nPLEASE PICK THE L.H. CORNER OF MONO HEAD "))
 (COMMAND "UCS" "O" P1)
 (SETQ P1 (LIST 0 0 0))
 (SETQ L (GETREAL "\nPLEASE ENTER THE HEAD LENGTH ")
       W (GETREAL "\nPLEASE ENTER THE HEAD WIDTH ")
       H (GETREAL "\nPLEASE ENTER THE HEAD HEIGHT ")
       ALP (/ (GETREAL "\nENTER THE FRONT ANGLE (DEG) ") (/ 180 PI))
       BET (/ (GETREAL "\nENTER THE SIDE ANGLE (DEG) ") (/ 180 PI))
       LM (* H (/ (SIN ALP)(COS ALP)))
       WM (* H (/ (SIN BET)(COS BET)))
       P2 (LIST L 0 0) P3 (LIST 0 W 0) P4 (LIST L W 0)
       P5 (LIST LM WM H)
       P6 (LIST LM (- (CADR P3) WM) H)
       P7 (LIST (CAR P2) WM H)
       P8 (LIST (CAR P4) (- (CADR P4) WM) H)
       P9 (LIST (/ LM 5)(/ WM 5)(- 0 (/ H 5)))
       P10 (LIST (CAR P2)(/ WM 5)(- 0 (/ H 5)))
       P11 (LIST (/ LM 5)(- (CADR P3)(/ WM 5))(- 0 (/ H 5)))
       P12 (LIST (CAR P4)(- (CADR P4) (/ WM 5))(- 0 (/ H 5))))
 (COMMAND "3DMESH" 5 3 P9 P1 P5 P10 P2 P7 P12 P4 P8 P11 P3 P6
                    P9 P1 P5
         "3DFACE" P5 P7 P8 P6 "" "UCS" "P")
 (COMMAND "UCS" "P")
 (SETVAR "CMDECHO" 1)
 (PRINC)
)
```

The program uses the basic rectangle (drawn from the points 'P1', 'P2', 'P3' and 'P4') which are taken from the length and width input values. The remaining points are calculated by means of the modified length ('LM') and width ('WM') resulting from the input values 'ALP' and 'BET' (see Figure 57).

Figure 57

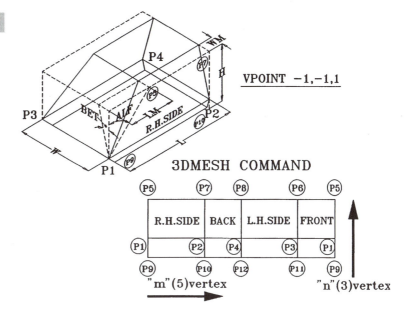

The programme uses the trigonometrical relationship:

$$\tan \alpha = \frac{\sin \alpha}{\cos \alpha}$$

Note also that the 3DMESH 'M' value becomes 5 (*not* 4) by repeating the first 'M' value to close the front face.

After running the program test by using the HIDE command followed by the command SHADE.

See if you can alter MONO.LSP by adding two new points to give a similar view to the one shown at the bottom of page 135. (**Hint**: Use an 'N' vertex value of 4.)

System variables

We have used two system variable functions to date, that of GETVAR and SETVAR. There is one more system variable we need to understand:

- **GETENV** – This function returns the string value assigned to a system environment variable. At the command prompt:

```
(GETENV "ACAD") Returns /ACAD/SUPPORT
(GETENV "ACADCFG") Returns \ACAD
```

These are only two more functions to cover to complete the requirements of the City & Guilds *AutoLISP Programming* scheme (C&G 4351–005):

▓ **WRITE-CHAR** – This function writes one character at a time to a previously opened external file: '(WRITE-CHAR <character> <file>)'. The character argument must be a number representing the ASCII code of the actual character that you wish to write to file:

```
(SETQ A (OPEN "TEST.DAT" "w"))
(WRITE-CHAR 115 A) Returns 115 but writes s to file TEST.DAT
(CLOSE A)
SHELL (Ref.: ACAD.PGP file)
TYPE TEST.DAT
```

Note the result. Now try to write 'G' to the file TEST.DAT by using the ASCII code 71.

▓ **READ-CHAR** – This function is the reverse of WRITE-CHAR; try to read the file TEST.DAT with the following command:

```
(READ-CHAR A)
```

But remember that the file must be opened before you can read from it.

Coda

Whilst there are more AutoLISP functions to learn, the two parts, *AutoLISP in Action* and *Advanced AutoLISP* cover far more than is necessary to reach the required City & Guilds AutoLISP Programming standard. These exercises have been restricted to the development of individually loaded programs and it must be remembered that AutoLISP forms an important role in the customisation of screen and 'pop-up' menus.

Problem 24
Intersections

I have chosen this problem because it is interesting to 'cut-out' the resultant development in paper to make a prototype. The problem involves the development of intersecting shapes, a subject covered by many specialist software vendors. As the objective of all my AutoLISP publications has been to encourage AutoCAD users to seek their own solutions to problems by using AutoLISP macros, here is such a solution for the intersection of a cone and cylinder (see Figure 58).

CTCINT.LSP

```
(DEFUN C:CTCINT () ; Cone To Cylinder INTersection
(GRAPHSCR)
 (SETQ D  (GETREAL "\nPLEASE ENTER THE CONE DIA. ")
      H  (GETREAL "\nENTER THE CONE VERTICAL HEIGHT TO APEX ")
      CH (GETREAL "\nENTER THE VERTICAL HEIGHT TO CYLINDER C.LINE")
      CD (GETREAL "\nENTER THE CYLINDER DIA. ")
      OC (GETREAL "\nENTER THE CYLINDER LENGTH TO THE CONE C.LINE ")
      A 0 DX 0 RAT (/ D H))
 (PROMPT "\nPICK THE CYLINDER DEVELOPMENT BOTTOM L.H.CORNER. ")
 (COMMAND "UCS" "O" PAUSE)
 (SETQ P1 (LIST 0 0))
 (DEFUN SUBR ()
  (SETQ X (* (/ CD 2)(COS A)) Y (* (/ CD 2)(SIN A))
       H1 (- H (+ CH Y)) R1 (/ (* RAT H1) 2)
       L1 (SQRT (- (* R1 R1)(* X X))))
 )
   (REPEAT 101 ; cylinder development
    (SUBR)
    (SETQ L (- OC L1) P2 (LIST DX L))
    (COMMAND "LINE" P1 P2 "")
    (SETQ P1 P2 A (+ A (/ PI 50)) DX (+ DX (/ (* PI CD) 100)))
   )
  (SETQ P3 (POLAR P1 (* 1.5 PI) L) P4 (POLAR P3 PI (* PI CD)))
  (COMMAND "LINE" P1 P3 P4 "" "UCS" "P")
  (PROMPT "\nPICK THE CONE DEVELOPMENT APEX POINT ")
  (COMMAND "UCS" "O" PAUSE)
  (SETQ P0 (LIST 0 0) A 0)
```

→

```
  (SETQ SH (SQRT (+ (* H1 H1)(* R1 R1)))
        Q (ATAN (/ X L1)) Q1 (/ (* Q R1) SH)
        P1 (POLAR P0 Q1 SH) A (/ PI 50))
  (REPEAT 100  ; cone cutout development
    (SUBR)
    (SETQ SH (SQRT (+ (* H1 H1)(* R1 R1)))
          Q (ATAN (/ X L1)) Q1 (/ (* Q R1) SH)
          P2 (POLAR P0 Q1 SH))
    (COMMAND "LINE" P1 P2 "")
    (SETQ P1 P2 A (+ A (/ PI 50)))
  )
  (SUBR)
  (SETQ SH (SQRT (+ (* H H)(* (/ D 2)(/ D 2))))
        RA (/ (* PI D) SH) ; cone base development
        P5 (POLAR P0 (- (/ RA 2)) SH)
        P6 (POLAR P0 (/ RA 2) SH))
    (COMMAND "LINE" P0 P5 "" "ARC" P5 "C" P0 P6 "LINE" P6 P0 "")
  (COMMAND "UCS" "P")
)
```

Figure 58

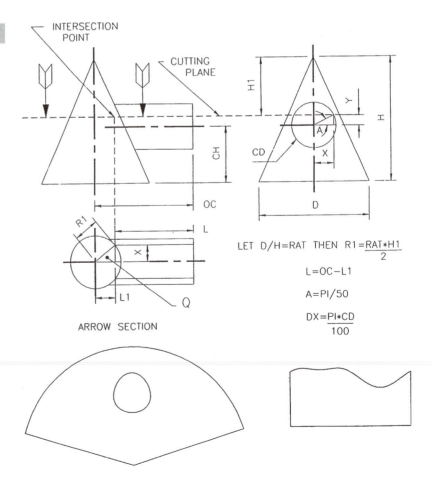

ARROW SECTION

LET D/H=RAT THEN R1=$\frac{RAT*H1}{2}$

L=OC−L1

A=PI/50

DX=$\frac{PI*CD}{100}$

If you are used to solving such problems by means of a pencil and drawing board you will know that the best solution to this type of problem is to make a series of cutting planes across the intersection line and to project the intersection point to the remaining views.

Consider a cutting plane (as in the Figure) taken at the intersection of a rotating radius at angle 'A' with the circumference 'CD' of the cylinder diameter. If this point is then projected to the two remaining views, the resultant geometry makes it possible to calculate the slant height ('SH') of the cone and the cylinder length ('L') for this particular intersection point.

If angle 'A' is rotated in stages through one complete revolution, a series of intersection points between the cone and the cylinder can be determined.

The program consists of three stages:

1. The development of the cylinder.
2. The cone cutout.
3. Cone base development.

Note the use of a sub-routine (SUBR) in the program, this is not essential and is of little benefit to the length of the program.

Run the program and test with a paper prototype.

You will have noticed the doing part of the program is within the repeat loops. This is deliberate as I wish you to edit the program to place the doing activities outside the loop.

Problem 25
A stitch in time

For a 'perfect cadence' I have chosen to finish with something very different. The program is in response to a request for a computer program for generating different patterns suitable for embroidery, to be used by people of limited computer skills.

KURVE.LSP

```
(DEFUN C:KURVE ()
  (GRAPHSCR)
  (SETVAR "CMDECHO" 0)(SETVAR "BLIPMODE" 0)
  (SETQ P1 (GETPOINT "PLEASE ENTER THE START POINT ")
        REC (GETDIST P1 "\nENTER NUMBER OF RECURSIONS ")
        ANG 0)
    (COMMAND "PLINE" P1)
     (REPEAT 4
       (SHAP REC ANG)
       (SETQ ANG (- ANG (/ PI 2)))
     )
    (COMMAND "")
  (SETVAR "CMDECHO" 1)(SETVAR "BLIPMODE" 1)
  (PRINC)
)
```

SHAP1.LSP

```
(DEFUN SHAP (A B)
  (IF (< A 1)
    (COMMAND (SETQ P1 (POLAR P1 B A)))
     (PROGN
       (SHAP (/ A 2.0) B)
       (SHAP (/ A 2.0)(+ B (/ PI 2)))
       (SHAP (/ A 2.0) B)
       (SHAP (/ A 2.0)(- B (/ PI 2)))
       (SHAP (/ A 2.0) B)
     )
   )
)
```

KURVE2.LSP

```
(DEFUN C:KURVE2 ()
 (GRAPHSCR)
  (SETVAR "CMDECHO" 0)(SETVAR "BLIPMODE" 0)
 (SETQ P1 (GETPOINT "PLEASE ENTER THE START POINT ")
      REC (GETDIST P1 "\nENTER NUMBER OF RECURSIONS ")
      ANG 0)
  (COMMAND "PLINE" P1)
   (REPEAT 4
    (SHAP2 REC ANG)
    (SETQ ANG (- ANG (/ PI 2)))
   )
  (COMMAND "")
  (SETVAR "CMDECHO" 1)(SETVAR "BLIPMODE" 1)
  (PRINC)
)
```

SHAP2.LSP

```
(DEFUN SHAP2 (A B)
 (IF (< A 1)
  (COMMAND (SETQ P1 (POLAR P1 B A)))
   (PROGN
    (SHAP2 (/ A 2.0) B)
    (SHAP2 (/ A 2.0)(+ B (/ PI 3)))
    (SHAP2 (/ A 2.0) B)
    (SHAP2 (/ A 2.0)(- B (/ PI 3)))
    (SHAP2 (/ A 2.0) B)
   )
  )
)
```

KURVE3.LSP

```
(DEFUN C:KURVE3 ()
 (GRAPHSCR)
  (SETVAR "CMDECHO" 0)(SETVAR "BLIPMODE" 0)
 (SETQ P1 (GETPOINT "PLEASE ENTER THE START POINT ")
      REC (GETDIST P1 "\nENTER NUMBER OF RECURSIONS ")
      ANG 0)
  (COMMAND "PLINE" P1)
   (REPEAT 8
    (SHAP3 REC ANG)
    (SETQ ANG (- ANG (/ PI 4)))
   )
  (SETVAR "CMDECHO" 1)(SETVAR "BLIPMODE" 1)
  (PRINC)
  (COMMAND "")
)
```

SHAP3.LSP

```
(DEFUN SHAP3 (A B)
 (IF (< A 1)
   (COMMAND (SETQ P1 (POLAR P1 B A)))
    (PROGN
     (SHAP3 (/ A 2.0) B)
     (SHAP3 (/ A 2.0)(+ B (/ PI 4)))
     (SHAP3 (/ A 2.0)(- B (/ PI 4)))
     (SHAP3 (/ A 2.0) B)
    )
   )
 )
```

Figure 59

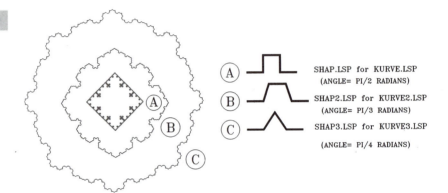

If the six programs are placed in the appropriate files, then all that is necessary to run the programs would be to enter at the keyboard: KURVE, KURVE2 or KURVE3.

Notice the use of three different basic shapes called SHAP, SHAP2 and SHAP3, why didn't I use the name SHAPE for the functions?

Alternatively, you could customise the AutoCAD menu to simplify the operation by simply highlighting the command on the screen and using a single 'pick'.

As simple menu customisation forms part of the City & Guilds *AutoLSIP Programming* assessment (C&G 4351–005), can I invite you to take the third rung of the ladder by progressing to Part Three *City & Guilds AutoLISP Programming*?

Exercises

1. Edit CYL.LSP to change the accuracy of the developed curve.
2. Edit CYL.LSP to automatically vary the accuracy of the curve to suit the value of the input radius.
3. Edit CYL.LSP to make use of the sub-routine degrees to radians.
4. Modify the ELEC2.LSP program to draw the resultant voltage from the input values of two out of phase sinusoidal voltages in an AC circuit.
5. Modify SUSP.LSP to determine the length of rope or chain required to form the CATENARY curve.
6. Change the RT.LSP program to construct text around an ellipse.
7. Edit the KNURL.LSP program to eliminate the need for preparatory drawing.
8. Design an AutoLISP macro to construct a disk-cam profile using a knife-edge follower, having a motion of uniform velocity over a 90° displacement.
9. Edit PURLIN4.LSP to make the program idiot-proof by controlling the keyboard input values.
10. Select any program using the READ-LINE function in a loop and use the logical operator NOT as a test condition to detect the end of a file and to close the file that has been used for reading.
11. Modify the MONO.LSP program to include the faces as shown in Figure 56.
12. Modify the CTCINT.LSP macro so that the doing part of the program is outside of the loop.

Note: The above questions do not reflect in any way the course assessment for the *AutoLISP Programming* certificate (C&G 4351–005) and in most cases set a higher standard.

Part Three
City & Guilds AutoLISP Programming

Introduction

This section covers the necessary AutoLISP routines for the City & Guilds 4351–005 scheme, and will be of practical use to all trainees whether they are following City & Guilds courses or not.

Having completed *AutoLISP in Action* and *Advanced AutoLISP* you should now be able to complete the log book which consists of the learning objectives (with the exception of customisation of menus, which will be covered in this section). A copy of the completed City & Guilds log book must be available for inspection for a period of eight weeks after application for the certificate has been made.

Assessment

The assessment is made up of *three* practical assignments *and* one written (multi-choice) test.

In order to obtain a certificate it will be necessary to enrole as an external student at a college running the City & Guilds *AutoCAD Programming* scheme (C&G 4351–005).

All four assessments will need to be conducted at a college at a time convenient to yourself and the college. It is advisable to arrange for each assignment to be undertaken at intervals of time, rather than all at once.

The assessment preparation consists of exercises designed to prepare you for the certificate and will consist of in the main questions and answers.

It should be remembered that there is often more than one correct solution to a particular problem in AutoLISP. The best solution is the one that suits you at the particular time and stage of your development. Hence the solutions are only suggestions to help you arrive at your own solutions.

This chapter is in four sections which represent the necessary skills and underpinning knowledge to enable the candidate to undertake the program of assessments for each of the four assignments.

I would not recommend leaving all your assessment until you complete the course of study.

City & Guilds course requirements

In the City & Guilds log book you are required to demonstrate that you understand and can use the following functions and features.

Using AutoLISP

System and interpreter requirements:

- Access and use AutoLISP on an AutoCAD system which has been configured to enable the use of AutoLISP.
- Set the LISPHEAP and LISPSTACK environment variables where necessary.
- Use and describe the purpose of the ACAD.LSP file.

Command line entry:

- Use '(...)' and '!' to enter an AutoCAD command to evaluate a simple, one line, LISP function and describe how the interpreter evaluator responds to incorrect expressions.
- Load and initiate a LISP routine at the AutoCAD command prompt.

Text editors:

- Explain the significance of producing pure ASCII mode files using text editors.
- Activate and use a text editor or wordprocessor from within, or outside of, the AutoCAD environment.

Program structure and presentation

Outline structure:

- Describe the outline structure of an AutoLISP program and how the evaluator deals with expressions and parenthesis.

Syntax:

- Describe and use the required conventions for symbol names and describe the lexical conventions for data input and the use of the characters:

```
( ) ' " ; \ space
```

■ Use and describe the purpose of *functions* and *arguments* and the difference between *global* and *local* variables.

Presentation:

■ Use upper and/or lower case consistently to improve program readability.
■ Use comments to improve understanding and facilitate maintenance of programs.
■ Indent text and use line breaks consistently to indicate the structure of the program and make it more readable.

Data types:

■ Use and describe the following data types: *symbols*, *strings*, *file descriptors*, *subroutines*.
■ Use and describe the following number data types: *real* numbers, *integers*.
■ Use the following special data types: *selection sets*, *entity name*.
■ Use and describe the data type *lists* and their assembly and disassembly.
■ Use and describe *quotes* as used for literal strings and the purpose of the backslash character control codes:

```
\n \t \r \nnn
```

■ Use and describe constants (special symbols) such as:

```
PI NIL T
```

AutoLISP functions and operators

Assignment:

■ Use and describe the purpose of the functions:

```
set setq
```

Arithmetic:

■ Use the following arithmetic functions:

```
+ - * /
```

■ Use and describe the purpose of the following increment-decrement and special functions:

```
1+ 1- sqrt expt rem
```

Relational operators:

■ Use the following relational functions:

```
= /= < <= > >=
```

Logical operators:

■ Use the following logical operators:

```
AND OR NOT
```

Creating functions:

■ Use and describe the DEFUN function to create new functions and the methods used to set global and local variables.

■ Use and describe the method by which the DEFUN function may be used to create new AutoCAD commands using names in the form C:NAME and automatic functions using names in the form S::NAME.

List functions:

■ Use and describe the list construction and checking functions:

```
APPEND ATOM CONS LIST
```

■ Use and describe the list extraction functions:

```
ASSOC CAR CDR CADR CADDR NTH LAST
```

■ Use and describe the list manipulation functions:

```
APPLY EVAL FOREACH SUBST REVERSE
```

Input and output:

■ Describe and use the following methods (functions) of controlling and obtaining user input:

```
GETANGLE GETCORNER GETDIST GETINT GETKWORD
GETORIENT GETPOINT GETREAL GETSTRING INITGET
```

■ Describe and use the following methods (functions) of printing output:

```
PRINL PRINT PRINC PROMPT
```

■ Use the TERPRI function to print a new line on the screen.

Conditions and control structures:

■ Use and describe the purpose of the control type functions COND and IF.
■ Use and describe the REPEAT, PROGN and WHILE functions.
■ Use and describe the predicate (test) functions:

```
ATOM BOUNDP EQ EQUAL LISTP NUMBERP NULL
```

String and conversion functions:

■ Use and describe the purpose of the functions:

```
ABS ANGTOS ATOF ATOI ASCII
CHR FIX FLOAT ITOA RTOS
```

■ Use and describe the string manipulation functions:

```
STRCASE STRCAT STRLEN SUBSTR
```

Database manipulation:

- Use and describe the purpose of the functions:

  ENTLAST ENTNEXT ENTSEL ENTGET ENTMOD ENTUPD

- Use and describe the purpose of the functions:

  SSGET SSLENGTH SSNAME

- Use filters with SSGET.

AutoCAD related functions:

- Use the following functions:

  GRAPHSCR REDRAW TEXTSCR

- Use and describe the COMMAND function.
- Use and describe the purpose of the functions:

  ANGLE DISTANCE INTERS POLAR

System variable manipulation:

- Use and describe the functions:

  GETENV GETVAR SETVAR

File handling:

- Use and describe the functions OPEN and CLOSE, and the methods used to read, write and append to files.
- Use the functions to read and write to files:

  WRITE-LINE READ-LINE READ-CHAR WRITE-CHAR

Programming

Simple routines:

- Write and execute AutoLISP programs for a variety of tasks.
- Write and use routines as part of a customised (specific) drawing package.
- Write and use AutoLISP macros in conjunction with AutoCAD menus.
- Write and use AutoLISP routines which incorporate AutoCAD commands.

Documentation:

- Produce documentation for the purpose of maintenance of program routines.
- Produce user documentation for the use of program routines.
- Produce annotated copy of program routines.

Practical assignment 1
(8 hours) .

Note: Each AutoLISP routine must be commented with explanatory details including your name and date of creation. It is also necessary to declare local variables such as '(/ P1 P2 RAD)' etc.; however, for simplicity I will exclude these features from my solutions.

Problem 1

To write an AutoLISP macro that draws a line of any length and direction having a check for 'null' input.

Solution

The solution is given in MYL.LSP

MYL.LSP

```
(DEFUN C:MYL ()
  (GRAPHSCR)
  (INITGET 1)
  (SETQ P1 (GETPOINT "PICK THE START POINT "))
  (INITGET 1)
  (SETQ P2 (GETPOINT "\nPICK THE END POINT "))
  (COMMAND "LINE" P1 P2 "")
   (PRINC)
)
```

Problem 2

Add to the above problem the need to include an extra line 10 units to the right-hand side of 'P1'–'P2' and another line 20 units to the left-hand side of 'P1'–'P2', both the new lines to be the dashed line type. Use the LINE, OFFSET and CHANGE commands.

Solution

The solution is given in MYL2.LSP

MYL2.LSP

```
(DEFUN C:MYL2 ()
 (GRAPHSCR)
 (INITGET 1)
 (SETQ P1 (GETPOINT "PICK THE START POINT "))
 (INITGET 1)
 (SETQ P2 (GETPOINT "\nPICK THE END POINT "))
  (COMMAND "LINE" P1 P2 ""
           "OFFSET" 10 P1 (POLAR P1 0 10) ""
           "CHANGE" "L" "" "P" "LT" "DASHED" ""
           "OFFSET" 20 P1 (POLAR P1 PI 10) ""
           "CHANGE" "L" "" "P" "LT" "DASHED" "")
 (PRINC)
)
```

Problem 3

Write an AutoLISP program to draw a line 29.87 units long from input values for start point and angle.

Solution

The solution is given in MYL3.LSP

MYL3.LSP

```
(DEFUN C:MYL3 ()
 (GRAPHSCR)
 (INITGET 1)
 (SETQ P1 (GETPOINT " PICK THE START POINT "))
 (INITGET 1)
 (SETQ A (GETANGLE "\nENTER THE ANGLE IN DEGREES ")
      P2 (POLAR P1 A 29.87))
  (COMMAND "LINE" P1 P2 "")
 (PRINC)
)
```

Problem 4

A program is required to complete the drawing shown in Figure 60. The program is required in three parts or three different routines: CROSS, FRONTF and CHURCH. CHURCH being the assembly of CROSS and FRONTF. The insertion point is as shown on the drawing and CROSS and FRONTF must be available as an input angle.

Figure 60

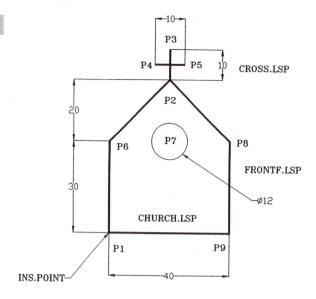

Solution

I have chosen a series of subroutines to save repetitive programming (you do not have to follow suit). There is a dimensional relationship between CROSS and FRONTF when assembled to form CHURCH, enabling the use of a temporary UCS origin at the insertion point 'P1':

- **ASSY.LSP** – This subroutine is common to all three final routines.
- **DRAW1.LSP** – This subroutine contains the necessary graphics to complete the CROSS.
- **DRAW2.LSP** – This is the last subroutine, containing the graphics necessary to draw the front face of the church.

CROSS.LSP

```
(DEFUN C:CROSS ()   ; FIRST ROUTINE
  (ASSY)
  (DRAW1)
  (COMMAND "UCS" "P")
  (PRINC)
)
```

FRONTF.LSP

```
(DEFUN C:FRONTF ()   ; SECOND ROUTINE
  (ASSY)
  (DRAW2)
  (COMMAND "UCS" "P")
  (PRINC)
)
```

CHURCH.LSP

```
(DEFUN C:CHURCH ()   ; THIRD ROUTINE
  (ASSY)
  (DRAW1)
  (DRAW2)
  (COMMAND "UCS" "P")
  (PRINC)
)
```

ASSY.LSP

```
(DEFUN ASSY ()   ;SUB-ROUTINE
  (GRAPHSCR)
  (INITGET 1)
  (SETQ P1 (GETPOINT "\nPLEASE PICK THE INSERTION POINT "))
  (COMMAND "UCS" "O" P1)
  (SETQ P1 (LIST 0 0))
  (INITGET 1)
  (SETQ A (GETREAL"\nPLEASE ENTER THE ANGLE IN DEGREES "))
)
```

DRAW1.LSP

```
(DEFUN DRAW1 ()    ; SUB-ROUTINE FOR CROSS
  (SETQ P2 (LIST 20 50) P3 (LIST 20 60)
       P4 (LIST 15 55) P5 (LIST 25 55))
  (COMMAND "LINE" P2 P3 "" "LINE" P4 P5 ""
       "ROTATE" "C" P1 P5 "" P1 A)
)
```

DRAW2.LSP

```
(DEFUN DRAW2 ()    ; SUB-ROUTINE FOR SOUTHFace
  (SETQ P6 (LIST 0 30) P7 (LIST 20 30)
       P8 (LIST 40 30) P9 (LIST 40 0))
  (COMMAND "PLINE" P1 P6 P2 P8 P9 "CLOSE"
       "CIRCLE" P7 6
       "ROTATE" "C" P1 P8 "" P1 A)
)
```

If by now you are a little tired of loading AutoLISP macros from the keyboard, why not use an AutoLISP program to simplify the process?

You may find LODE.LSP useful, note that we could not name it 'LOAD' since this is an existing AutoLISP function.

LODE.LSP

```
(DEFUN  C:LODE  ()     ;LOAD LISP
  (SETQ FUNCT (GETSTRING "ENTER THE AUTOLISP FILE TO LOAD "))
   (LOAD FUNCT)
)
```

Remember to load the program before use. Type LODE at the command prompt followed by the name of the AutoLISP macro that you wish to load.

Problem 5

Write an AutoLISP routine to produce the drawing shown in Figure 61, with a 3DFACE on all four sides, having picked the start point.

Figure 61

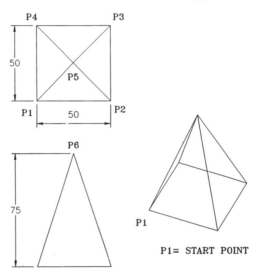

Solution

The solution is given in 3DPYR.LSP

3DPYR.LSP

```
(DEFUN  C:3DPYR  () ;PYRamid
  (GRAPHSCR)
  (INITGET 1)
  (SETQ P1 (GETPOINT "PICK THE INSERTION POINT ")
        P2  (POLAR P1 0 50) P3 (POLAR P2 (/ PI 2) 50)
        P4  (POLAR P1 (/ PI 2) 50) P5 (INTERS P1 P3 P2 P4)
        P6  (LIST (CAR P5)(CADR P5) 75)
  )
  (COMMAND "3DFACE" P1 P2 P6 "" ""
          "ARRAY" "L" "" "P" P6 4 "" "")
  (PRINC)
)
```

Problem 6

Write a macro that selects the boundaries by picking the intersections 'P1' and 'P2' and automatically trims the lines as shown in Figure 62.

Figure 62

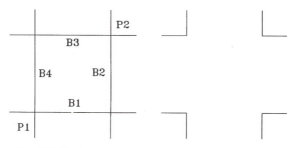

P= POINT, B= BOUNDARY

Solution

The solution is given in CROSSING.LSP

CROSSNG.LSP

```
(DEFUN C:CROSSING ()
  (GRAPHSCR)
  (SETVAR "OSMODE" 32)
  (SETQ P1 (GETPOINT "PICK THE BOTTOM L.H.INTERSECTION ")
        P2 (GETPOINT "\nPICK THE TOP R.H.INTERSECTION "))
  (SETVAR "OSMODE" 0)
   (SETQ DIS (DISTANCE P1 P2)
         B1 (POLAR P1 0 (/ DIS 2))
         B2 (POLAR P2 (* 1.5 PI)(/ DIS 2))
         B3 (POLAR P2 PI (/ DIS 2))
         B4 (POLAR P1 (/ PI 2)(/ DIS 2))
   )
   (COMMAND "TRIM" B1 B2 B3 B4 "" B1 B2 B3 B4"")
  (PRINC)
)
```

Problem 7

Refer to Problem 12 in *Advanced AutoLISP*, page 83. This problem involved extracting attributes from a drawing WBLOCK and writing this data to an external file.

We will use this macro ATTE.LSP to help solve the problem of extracting attribute data and displaying this data (as shown below) on the screen similar to the drawing using a single pick point activation.

```
                              NORTH YORK DEVELOPMENTS LTD.
                              ADDRESS of PROPERTY.....51 George Street
                                                      Bickley
                                                      nil
                                                      BR1 5ZY
                              LOCATION ...............Bromley
                              TYPE of PROPERTY........Bungalow
                              NUMBER of ROOMS.........5
                              AGE of PROPERTY.........110 YEARS
```

Solution

The solution is given in ATTE3.LSP

ATTE3.LSP

```lisp
(DEFUN C:ATTE3 ()
 (SETQ SS (CAR (ENTSEL "PLEASE PICK THE BLOCK "))
       EN (ENTNEXT SS)
       ATT1 (CDR (ASSOC 1 (ENTGET EN))) ;BUNGALOW
       EN (ENTNEXT EN)
       ATT2 (CDR (ASSOC 1 (ENTGET EN ))) ;BROMLEY
       EN (ENTNEXT EN)
       ATT3 (CDR (ASSOC 1 (ENTGET EN ))) ;51 GEORGE STREET
       EN (ENTNEXT EN)
       ATT4 (CDR (ASSOC 1 (ENTGET EN ))) ;BICKLEY
       EN (ENTNEXT EN)
       ATTS (CDR (ASSOC 1 (ENTGET EN ))) ;KENT
       EN (ENTNEXT EN)
       ATT6 (CDR (ASSOC 1 (ENTGET EN ))) ;110
       EN (ENTNEXT EN)
       ATT7 (CDR (ASSOC 1 (ENTGET EN ))) ;BR1 5ZY
       EN (ENTNEXT EN)
       ATT8 (CDR (ASSOC 1 (ENTGET EN ))) ;5
 )
 (TEXTSCR)
 (TERPRI)
 (PRINC "\t\tNORTH YORK DEVELOPMENTS LTD.")
 (TERPRI)
 (PRINC "\t\tADDRESS of PROPERTY......")(PRINC ATT3)(TERPRI)
 (PRINC "\t\t                         ")(PRINC ATT4)(TERPRI)
 (PRINC "\t\t                         ")(PRINC ATT5)(TERPRI)
 (PRINC "\t\t                         ")(PRINC ATT7)(TERPRI)
 (PRINC "\t\tLOCATION ................")(PRINC ATT2)(TERPRI)
 (PRINC "\t\tTYPE of PROPERTY.........")(PRINC ATT1)(TERPRI)
 (PRINC "\t\tNUMBER of ROOMS..........")(PRINC ATT8)(TERPRI)
 (PRINC "\t\tAGE of PROPERTY..........")(PRINC ATT6)(PRINC"\tYEARS")
 (PRINC)
)
```

See page 71 of *Advanced AutoLISP* and relate this to ATTE3.LSP, noting that the 'select – get – search – do' part of the program is repeated eight times before doing something.

Select   (ENTNEXT ...)
Get   (ENTGET ...) *performed eight times*
Search   (CDR (ASSOC 1 ...))
Do   (PRINC ...)

In order to test the program you must produce a WBLOCK with the attributes shown in Problem 12 *Advanced AutoLISP*, page 83. Insert the WBLOCK into the drawing editor, load and run ATTE3.LSP.

There may be a temptation for you to insert the TEXTSCR function at the top of the program as we have been doing with the GRAPHSCR function. That would cause problems as it must follow the ENTSEL function if the program is to toggle from GRAPHSCREEN to TEXTSCREEN after picking the WBLOCK.

Problem 8

Write an AutoLISP macro which allows the user to correct the spelling mistakes shown in the text in Figure 63. Produce the text within the AutoCAD drawing editor before running the AutoLISP macro.

Figure 63

THIS IS AN EXAPLE TEXT
IN NEED OF CORRICTION
PRODUCED INN AUTOCAD

Solution

See *Advanced AutoLISP*, page 105 – CHT.LSP is a macro that permits the editing of an AutoCAD text string without the need to correct the entire line.

Problem 9

Create an AutoLISP macro that imports text (from the external file WPT.TXT) into the drawing editor, with a text height of 6 units and a line spacing of 10 units.

Solution

See *Advanced AutoLISP*, page 92 – the solution is given in WPT.LSP. Create the file WPT.TXT and enter two lines of text. Load and run the macro.

WPT.LSP

```
(DEFUN C:WPT ()
 (GRAPHSCR)
 (SETQ P1 (GETPOINT "PICK THE TEXT START POINT ")
       P2 (LIST (CAR P1)(- (CADR P1) 10))
       FILE (OPEN "WPT.TXT" "r")
       LINE1 (READ-LINE FILE)
       LINE2 (READ-LINE FILE)
 )
 (CLOSE FILE)
 (COMMAND "TEXT" P1 "6" "0" LINE1
          "TEXT" P2 "6" "0" LINE2)
 (PRINC)
)
```

Conclusion

That completes the first assessment which must be undertaken within eight hours (not necessarily in one sitting). You do not require 100 per cent success to qualify for a 'pass'; it is possible to fail the last two problems and still pass the assignment. Remember to include comments and your name in all your AutoLISP programs. You will also be expected to declare all local variables within the program and to include any appropriate input checks.

Practical assignment 2
(3 hours)

Problem 1

Write an AutoLISP routine to draw a variable sized panel (see Figure 64).
    The user picks the bottom left-hand corner ('P1'), top right-hand corner ('P2') and enters the required number of equally spaced rows inside the panel.

Figure 64

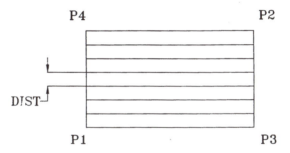

Solution

I think the simplest solution is to use the existing AutoCAD commands at all times, hence the use of the ARRAY command to draw the horizontal lines. You could use an AutoLISP loop function and re-calculate the end points of the lines within the loop if you so wish. (But there is no point in re-inventing the wheel!)

PANEL.LSP

```
(DEFUN C:PANEL ()
 (GRAPHSCR)
 (SETQ P1 (GETPOINT "PICK THE LOWER L.H.CORNER ")
       P2 (GETCORNER P1 "PICK THE TOP R.H.CORNER ")
       P3 (LIST (CAR P2)(CADR P1))
       P4 (LIST (CAR P1)(CADR P2))
       NUMB (GETINT "\nENTER THE NUMBER OF ROWS ")
       DIST (/ (DISTANCE P1 P4) NUMB)
 )
 (COMMAND "LINE" P1 P4 P2 P3 "C"
          "ARRAY" (POLAR P1 0 5) "" "R" NUMB 1 DIST)
 (PRINC)
)
```

Problem 2

This involves the same problem as above, however the loading (if necessary) and running of the program has to be performed from a pull-down menu. The basic menu structure is provided, all you have to do is some very simple editing.

Solution

The unedited menu is shown below:

```
***BUTTONS
;
^C^C
^C^C
***POP1
[PANEL ROUTINE]
[================]
[Select number ]
[from list below ]
[to draw table ]
[automatically ]
[================]
[    2]^C^C
[    3]^C^C
[    4]^C^C
[    5]^C^C
[    6]^C^C
[    7]^C^C
[    8]^C^C
***SCREEN
[=======]
[AutoCAD]
[=======]
[ASST 2]
[panel]
[menu]
[=====]
[See POP1]
[menu]
```

Menu files are divided into sections relating to specific areas of the screen:

■ ***BUTTONS** – The button menu of the pointing device; there is no requirement for change in this case.

■ *****POP1** – Pull-down area of the screen, this is where our AutoLISP routines will appear.
■ *****SCREEN** – Screen menu area (right-hand side); again, there is no requirement for change in this case.

Using 'Ctrl+C' to cancel macros

Most command macros start with two or three '^C's. In a menu the 'Ctrl+C' keystroke combination is a special code that cancels a command. Because you want your AutoLISP functions to execute from the AutoCAD command prompt, starting a macro with three 'Ctrl+C's ensures that any existing command is cancelled in preparation for the AutoLISP function that follows.

Labelling macro commands

Look at the menu items; notice the characters inside square brackets. The contents of the square brackets are displayed to the screen.

If we use (SETQ NUMB ...) to match the screen value, pick and then execute the PANEL routine, there will be no need to input 'NUMB' within the PANEL.LSP program. Hence I have edited PANEL.LSP to PANEL2.LSP (removing the 'NUMB').

PANEL2.LSP

```
(DEFUN C:PANEL2 ()
 (GRAPHSCR)
 (SETQ P1 (GETPOINT "PICK THE LOWER L.H.CORNER ")
      P2 (GETCORNER P1 "PICK THE TOP R.H.CORNER ")
      P3 (LIST (CAR P2)(CADR P1))
      P4 (LIST (CAR P1)(CADR P2))
      DIST (/ (DISTANCE P1 P4) NUMB)
 )
 (COMMAND "LINE" P1 P4 P2 P3 "C"
         "ARRAY" (POLAR P1 0 5) "" "R" NUMB 1 DIST)
 (PRINC)
)
```

The edited menu is shown in PANEL.MNU

PANEL.MNU

```
***BUTTONS
;
^C^C
^C^C
***POP1
[PANEL ROUTINE]
[================ ]                                              ➡
```

```
←
[Select number    ]
[from list below  ]
[to draw table    ]
[automatically    ]
[================ ]
[    2]^C^C(SETQ NUMB 2);(IF (NOT PANEL2)(LOAD"PANEL2"));PANEL2
[    3]^C^C(SETQ NUMB 3);(IF (NOT PANEL2)(LOAD"PANEL2"));PANEL2
[    4]^C^C(SETQ NUMB 4);(IF (NOT PANEL2)(LOAD"PANEL2"));PANEL2
[    5]^C^C(SETQ NUMB 5);(IF (NOT PANEL2)(LOAD"PANEL2"));PANEL2
[    6]^C^C(SETQ NUMB 6);(IF (NOT PANEL2)(LOAD"PANEL2"));PANEL2
[    7]^C^C(SETQ NUMB 7);(IF (NOT PANEL2)(LOAD"PANEL2"));PANEL2
[    8]^C^C(SETQ NUMB 8);(IF (NOT PANEL2)(LOAD"PANEL2"));PANEL2
***SCREEN
[======]
[AutoCAD]
[======]
[ASST 2]
[panel]
[menu]
[=====]
[See POP1]
[menu]
```

Take care to delete any MNX files (as necessary) if you need to edit a MNU file prior to using the edited menu. When editing a MNU file for AutoCAD Release 13 for Windows, I still find it convenient to enter MENU at the command prompt and type in the menu file to load; this will re-compile the edited version automatically by saving the new source file (MNS) and recompiling the MNC and MNR files. Alternatively, you could use the MENULOAD and MENUUNLOAD commands. If you cannot remember the current menu name, try entering the command MENUNAME.

Note the use of semi-colons within PANEL.MNU. These semi-colons act as an 'Enter' key-press to each function or command in the menu. The first function is to set the value of the variable 'NUMB'. The second function tests to see if the AutoLISP macro is loaded. The test condition either loads the macro or does nothing, and then executes the new command PANEL2. There is no need to enter a semi-colon at the end of a line, since AutoLISP automatically places a space at the end of each completed line. The space has the same effect as a semi-colon.

Problem 3

This involves the insertion of symbols containing attributes into an existing line diagram. The line diagram will be provided, you will be expected to use two existing blocks within your AutoLISP macro. (See Figure 65.)

Input details:

1. Pick an insertion point.
2. Pick a second point to determine the angle required. (OSNAP must be set to 'nearest' for the above.)
3. Enter block name. (Attribute dialogue box disabled.)

When the macro runs, the attribute numbers must be displayed on the drawing, starting at number one, and incrementing by one as each new block is inserted. A gap, the actual length of the inserted symbol, must be removed from the line diagram prior to the required symbol being inserted.

Solution

We have already solved such a problem in *Advanced AutoLISP* – see page 107 (BOUT.LSP).

You will have to create two WBLOCKS (as shown in Figure 65) in order to test your solution (this will not be necessary when being assessed). Both blocks have two attributes as shown ('ITEM_NO' and 'VALUE'). Do not allocate any default values to these attributes; include a prompt for the tag 'VALUE' only.

When creating your WBLOCK select the tags in the following order: 'ITEM_NO', 'VALUE'; then save the WBLOCKS to your working directory. If you wish to insert the BLOCKS from a floppy disk then remember to edit the AutoLISP macro accordingly.

Edit BOUT.LSP as shown below to create BOUT2.LSP.

BOUT2.LSP

```
(DEFUN C:BOUT2 ()    ; Break OUT NO.2
  (GRAPHSCR)
  (SETVAR "OSMODE" 512)(SETVAR "ATTDIA" 0)
    (SETQ COUNT 1 P1 T)
    (WHILE P1
     (SETQ P1 (GETPOINT "\nPICK INSERTION POINT "))
     (SETQ A (GETANGLE P1 "\nPICK 2nd POINT of BREAK-OUT "))
            (INITGET 1 "Resistor Lamp")
            (SETQ B (GETKWORD "\nENTER THE BLOCK NAME R or L "))
            (INITGET 1)
            (SETQ ATT (GETSTRING "\nPLEASE ENTER COMPONENT VALUE "))
            (COND
              ((= B "Resistor")(SETQ GAP 30))
              ((= B "Lamp")(SETQ GAP 18))
            )
              (SETQ P2 (POLAR P1 A GAP)
                   AD (* A (/ 180 PI)))
              (COMMAND "BREAK" P1 P2
                      "INSERT" B P1 "" "" AD COUNT ATT)                      ➡
```

```
            (SETQ COUNT (1+ COUNT))
            (INITGET 1 "C E")
       (SETQ TEST (GETKWORD "\nENTER C TO CONTINUE E TO END "))
            (IF (= TEST "E")(SETQ P1 NIL))
   )                ;END WHILE
  (SETVAR "OSMODE" 0)
  (PRINC)
)
```

Figure 65

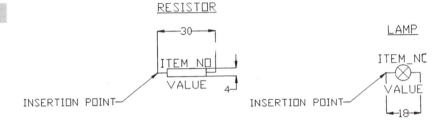

This completes the second practical assignment; it has to be completed in three hours. When you feel confident that you have achieved satisfactory competences in simple customisation of existing menus, and the necessary AutoLISP functions to insert symbols into an existing line with the necessary 'break out' (including the control of attributes within the WBLOCK), contact a College to arrange a suitable date and time for assessment.

Practical assignment 3
(3 hours)

The third assignment consists of a series of choices from two basic options:

- **Option 1** – External file manipulation
  Part A – Select *one* from *four*
  Part B – Select *one* from *four*

  or

- **Option 2** – Accessing the drawing database
  Select *one* from *four*

Option 1 – Part A

This involves reading a series of points from an external data file and performing some form of 'doing' by means of an AutoLISP routine. The doing part of the program involves either drawing lines between the points, drawing circles at the centre of these points, or using the TEXT command to print to screen these points.

Solution

We have read from an external file and drawn lines between each point in *Advanced AutoLISP* (see page 92).

Using the data files PTS2.DAT. I will solve the problem for drawing a series of circles and for writing text.

PTS2.DAT

```
43.23,124.27
146.21,33.82
250.41,116.81
367.89,118.35
359.06,259.53
210.21,270.86
149.06,222.22
125.45,191.77
71.96,192.52
C
```

Figure 66

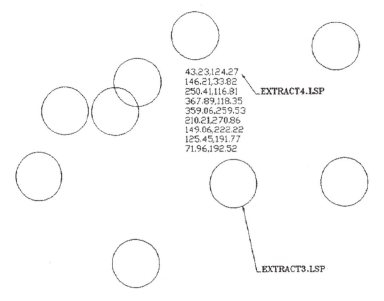

43,23,124.27
146.21,33.82
250.41,116.81
367.89,118.35
359.06,259.53
210.21,270.86
149.06,222.22
125.45,191.77
71.96,192.52

EXTRACT4.LSP

EXTRACT3.LSP

Figure 66 shows a series of circles (diameter: 50 units) whose centre points are read from the external file PTS2.DAT. You will need to create this data file and locate it in your working directory. The AutoLISP macro EXTRACT3.LSP reads the data file and draws the circles. This program is a modification of EXTRACT2.LSP which draws a line between each point in the external database (*Advanced AutoLISP* – see page 93).

EXTRACT3.LSP

```
(DEFUN C:EXTRACT3 ()
 (GRAPHSCR)
  (SETQ FILE (OPEN "PTS.DAT" "r") ; OPEN FILE
        PTS (READ-LINE FILE)      ; READ THE FIRST LINE
  )
   (WHILE PTS                ; LOOP UNTIL NIL IS RETURNED
    (COMMAND "CIRCLE" PTS 25)
    (SETQ PTS (READ-LINE FILE))
     (IF (EQ PTS "C")(SETQ PTS NIL))
         PTS (CONS LINE PTS))  ; ADD NEW LINE TO LIST
   )
   (CLOSE FILE)
   (PRINC)
)
```

EXTRACT4.LSP is a further modification to print to the screen using the TEXT command all the points in the external datafile. You will be asked to write an AutoLISP macro that either draws lines, draws circles or prints the coordinate points to the screen.

EXTRACT4.LSP

```
(DEFUN  C:EXTRACT4 ()
 (GRAPHSCR)
  (SETQ FILE (OPEN "PTS2.DAT" "r") ; OPEN FILE
        PTS (READ-LINE FILE)        ; READ THE FIRST LINE
        Y 220 P1 (LIST 200 Y)
  )
   (WHILE PTS                ; LOOP UNTIL NIL IS RETURNED
     (COMMAND "TEXT" P1 6 0 PTS)
     (SETQ PTS (READ-LINE FILE))
     (SETQ Y (- Y 10) P1 (LIST 200 Y))
      (IF(EQ PTS "C")(SETQ PTS NIL))
   )
   (CLOSE FILE)
   (PRINC)
)
```

Option 1 – Part B

This involves writing details to an external file. Part of the details involve accessing certain AutoCAD variables. You will be asked to write one of four possible AutoCAD variables to an external file. For simplicity I will combine all four different macros to give every possibility in one AutoLISP program.

The routine must ask the user for a name (which is then converted to upper case), access the drawing variables, and display the file to screen with a request for these details to be directed to an external file ('yes' or 'no').

Solution

The solution is given in EXPORT.LSP.

EXPORT.LSP

```
(DEFUN  C:EXPORT ()
 (GRAPHSCR)
 (SETQ ACCESS1 (GETVAR "DWGNAME")
       ACCESS2 (RTOS(GETVAR "CDATE"))
       NAM (STRCASE (GETSTRING 1 "ENTER YOUR NAME "))
       YEAR (SUBSTR ACCESS2 1 4)
       MONTH (SUBSTR ACCESS2 5 2)
       DAY (SUBSTR ACCESS2 7 2)
       TIME (SUBSTR ACCESS2 10 4)
       STR1 (STRCAT "DRAWING NAME: " ACCESS1)
       STR2 (STRCAT "DRAWN BY: " NAM)
       STR3 (STRCAT "YEAR: " YEAR)
       STR4 (STRCAT "MONTH: " MONTH)                          ➡
```

```
        STR5 (STRCAT "DAY: " DAY)
        STR6 (STRCAT "TIME: " TIME)
  )
  (TEXTSCR)
  (TERPRI)
  (PROMPT "    INFORMATION TO BE WRITTEN TO FILE: ")
  (TERPRI)
  (PROMPT "   ====================================")
  (TERPRI)
  (PROMPT "    ")(PRINC STR1)(TERPRI)
  (PROMPT "    ")(PRINC STR2)(TERPRI)
  (PROMPT "    ")(PRINC STR3)(TERPRI)
  (PROMPT "    ")(PRINC STR4)(TERPRI)
  (PROMPT "    ")(PRINC STR5)(TERPRI)
  (PROMPT "    ")(PRINC STR6)(TERPRI)
  (TERPRI)
  (PROMPT "   ====================================")
   (INITGET 1 "Yes No")
(SETQ REQ (GETKWORD "\nPERMISSION TO WRITE TO REPORT.TXT (Y or N) "))
   (IF (EQ REQ "Yes")(PROGN
            (SETQ FILE (OPEN "REPORT.TXT" "w"))
            (WRITE-LINE STR1 FILE)
            (WRITE-LINE STR2 FILE)
            (WRITE-LINE STR3 FILE)
            (WRITE-LINE STR4 FILE)
            (WRITE-LINE STR5 FILE)
            (WRITE-LINE STR6 FILE)
                    )
    )
  (CLOSE FILE)
  (PRINC)
)
```

Remember that you will only be expected to access one of the 'CDATE' variables in the City & Guilds *AutoCAD Programming* assessment (C&G 4351–005).

Problems 1 and 2 of this assignment must be completed within three hours if you choose Option 1.

Option 2

There are four options to this assignment; one will be selected by the assessor at random. All options require you to write an AutoLISP routine which accesses and modifies the drawing database. The problem would appear to suit architectural students.

Remember that you are expected to annotate all your AutoLISP macros giving explanations for important steps in the program. Test conditions should be included as appropriate.

Solution

In order to test your routine, create a drawing similar to Figure 67.

1. Set the drawing units to 'architectural', with $^1/_8$ as the smallest fraction.
2. Create four different layers in different colours named 'Wall', 'Column', 'Text' and 'Dimens'.
3. Create the drawing having entities placed on the relevantly named layers, using the LINE, CIRCLE, TEXT and DIMENSION commands. The circles on the 'Column' layer have a 16-inch diameter, with the exception of the two central columns, which have a 20-inch diameter
4. Save as PLAN.DWG.

Figure 67

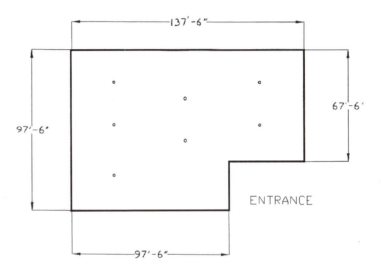

Choice 1

You have three hours to complete these four tasks. Remember when timing yourself that you will not be expected to produce the original drawing.

1. Write an AutoLISP program that creates a selection set of all circles on 'Column' layer.
2. Modify the association list to place all these circles in the zero layer and update the drawing. You must *not* use AutoCAD commands to achieve this.
3. Calculate the total area of the circles in square inches and print this value to the screen (again without using AutoCAD commands to calculate the area).
4. On satisfactory testing of the program, copy the AutoLISP macro to the ACAD.LSP file.

See *AutoLISP in Action*, page 76, for help with the (SSGET "X") function. See also *Advanced AutoLISP*, page 73, for further help.

CIRCL.LSP

```
(DEFUN C:CIRCL () ; SIMILAR TO PL.LSP
 (GRAPHSCR)
 (SETQ SS (SSGET "X" (LIST(CONS 0 "CIRCLE")(CONS 8 "COLUMN")))
       N (SSLENGTH SS)
       INDEX 0 TAREA 0
       P1 (GETPOINT "\nPICK THE LOCATION FOR TOTAL AREA ")
 )
  (REPEAT N
   (SETQ EL (ENTGET (SSNAME SS INDEX))
         MEL (SUBST (CONS 8 "0")(CONS 8 "COLUMN") EL))
   (ENTMOD MEL)
   (SETQ RAD (CDR (ASSOC 40 EL))
         ARE (* PI RAD RAD)
         TAREA (+ ARE TAREA)      ;Total AREA
         INDEX (1+ INDEX)
   )
  )
    (COMMAND "TEXT" P1 5 0 (RTOS TAREA 2 2))
    (PRINC)
)
```

This program selects all the circles on layer column in a selection set 'SS' (notice the use of the function LIST in conjunction with (SSGET "X").

Within the loop 'N' (the number of selected entities in the set) counts the selection set names via the ENTGET function and updates the information using the SUBST command:

```
(SUBST <new-list> <old-list> <assoc-list>)
       ➥(8. "0)    ➥(8. "COLUMN")    ➥EL
```

With different releases of AutoCAD currently in use you may have problems locating the ACAD.LSP file. If this is the case then create your own ACAD.LSP file and locate it in the 'ACAD' directory. This file is read whenever you load AutoCAD, making it possible to automatically load into all your drawing editors your favourite AutoLISP macros. This being the case you should only include in the ACAD.LSP file AutoLISP macros that are frequently used; all other AutoLISP macros should be loaded on demand.

1. Open a file called ACAD.LSP.
2. At the command prompt: `(LOAD "CIRCL")` and/or any other function you wish to load.
3. Locate your CIRCL.LSP and/or any other function in the working directory.
4. Access the AutoCAD drawing editor.
5. The AutoLISP file (or files) should be automatically loaded. Test this by entering the name of the function.

Choice 2

1. Write an AutoLISP program that creates a selection set containing all the lines on the 'Wall' layer.
2. Modify the associated list to place all the walls on the zero layer and update the drawing. You must not use AutoCAD commands to achieve this.
3. Calculate the cumulative length of these lines and print the answer to a selected point on the screen (in feet and inches) using the AutoCAD TEXT command,

LIN.LSP

```
(DEFUN C:LIN ()         ; SIMILAR TO CIRCL.LSP
 (GRAPHSCR)
 (SETQ SS (SSGET "X" (LIST(CONS 0 "LINE")(CONS 8 "WALL")))
       N (SSLENGTH SS)
       INDEX 0 TLEN 0
       P1 (GETPOINT "\nPICK THE LOCATION FOR TOTAL LENGTH ")
 )
  (REPEAT N
   (SETQ EL (ENTGET (SSNAME SS INDEX))
         MEL (SUBST (CONS 8 "0")(CONS 8 "WALL") EL))
   (ENTMOD MEL)
   (SETQ SPOINT (CDR (ASSOC 10 EL)) ;Start POINT
         EPOINT (CDR (ASSOC 11 EL)) ;End POINT
         LENGTH (DISTANCE SPOINT EPOINT)
         TLEN (+ LENGTH TLEN) ;Total LENgth
         INDEX (1+ INDEX)
   )
  )
    (COMMAND "TEXT" P1 5 0 (RTOS TLEN 4 2))
    (PRINC)
)
```

Notice the use of the special RTOS codes.

Load the drawing PLAN.DWG and run the AutoLISP macro. You should notice all the walls change colour to white, confirming the move to the zero layer, with the total length in the desired format displayed at point 'P1' on the screen.

Choice 3

1. Write an AutoLISP program that creates a selection set containing all text items on the 'Text' layer.
2. Modify the associated list to place the text items upside-down and update the drawing.

3. Calculate the total number of characters in the selection set (excluding spaces) and print the answer to a selected point on the screen using the AutoCAD TEXT command.

TEX.LSP

```
(DEFUN C:TEX ()
 (GRAPHSCR)
 (SETQ SS (SSGET "X" (LIST(CONS 0 "TEXT")(CONS 8 "TEXT")))
       N (SSLENGTH SS)
       INDEX 0 TSTRL 0 COUNT 1
       P1 (GETPOINT "\nPICK THE LOCATION FOR NO. OF CHARACTERS")
 )
  (REPEAT N
    (SETQ EL (ENTGET (SSNAME SS INDEX))
          MEL (SUBST (CONS 71 4)(CONS 71 0) EL))
    (ENTMOD MEL)
    (SETQ STR (CDR (ASSOC 1 EL))
          STRL (STRLEN STR))
        (REPEAT STRL
          (SETQ SEARCH (SUBSTR STR COUNT 1))
            (IF(/= SEARCH " ")(SETQ TSTRL (1+ TSTRL)))
            (SETQ COUNT (1+ COUNT))
        )
    (SETQ INDEX (1+ INDEX) COUNT 1)
  )
    (COMMAND "TEXT" P1 5 0 (ITOA TSTRL))
    (PRINC)
)
```

The DXF code '71' identifies the text generation:

0 = Normal
2 = Mirrored
4 = Upside down

The SUBSTR function searches the string 'STR' for the existence of characters (not spaces) for a length of one, adding the incremental COUNT value to the total string length 'TSTRL'.

Note the use of a nested loop, also the integer-to-string function ITOA.

Choice 4

1. Write an AutoLISP programme that creates a selection set containing all the dimensions in the drawing.
2. Modify the association list to change all the dimensions to layer zero and update the drawing (must not use the standard AutoCAD commands).
3. Convert the dimensions to millimetres using a multiple of 25.4 and update the drawing.

DIMN.LSP

```
(DEFUN C:DIMN ()
 (GRAPHSCR)
 (SETQ SS (SSGET "X" (LIST(CONS 0 "DIMENSION"))))
       N (SSLENGTH SS)
       INDEX 0)
  (REPEAT N
   (SETQ EL (ENTGET (SSNAME SS INDEX))
        MEL (SUBST (CONS 8 "0")(CONS 8 "DIMENS") EL))
   (ENTMOD MEL)
   (SETQ INDEX (1+ INDEX))
  )
    (SETVAR "DIMLFAC" 25.4)
    (COMMAND "UNITS" 2 2 1 2 0 "N"
            "DIM" "UPDATE" SS "" "EXIT")
    (PRINC)
)
```

Notice the use of the system variable 'DIMLFAC'. This is a global scale factor for linear dimensions. All such dimensions are multiplied by this factor.

The UNITS command is used to convert imperial dimensions to metric; these dimensions need to be 'associative' for this command to work within the AutoLISP macro.

Consideration should also be given to re-setting the above values after use.

Note: This completes the four choices for the alternative third practical assessment. You may wish to combine the third assessment with the following written paper.

Revision notes

Error handling

AutoLISP provides functions for error handling, these being:

```
ALERT *ERROR* EXIT QUIT
```

Correct use of the *ERROR* function will ensure that AutoCAD returns to a particular state in the event of an error. This is a user-defined function which returns the condition to the original state giving a screen message to the user.

For instance, consider an AutoLISP routine which changes certain SETVAR values at the start of the program, and restores them on completion of the program. If a 'Ctrl+C' key-press is made during the 'doing' stage of the program, the original SETVAR values will not be restored. AutoCAD calls the currently defined *ERROR* function and passes it an argument, which is a text string describing the nature of the error.

Your *ERROR* function should be designed to exit quietly after an exit function call.

The following function is the same as the standard AutoLISP error handler:

```
(DEFUN *ERROR* (MSG)
 (PRINC "ERROR:")
 (PRINC MSG)
 (PRINC)
)
```

This prints 'ERROR' to the screen with a description; note the 'clean' exit.

Consider a particular AutoLISP routine which sets the OSNAP mode to 'intersection'. The following function should be included at the start of the program to handle any error which may occur:

```
(DEFUN *ERROR* (MSG)    Defines new error function
 (SETVAR "OSMODE" 0)    Restores the condition
 (PRINC MSG)            Prints the type of error message
 (PRINC)                Exits cleanly
)
```

AutoLISP evaluator process

When AutoCAD receives some AutoLISP code, it passes that code to the AutoLISP interpreter. At the core of the AutoLISP interpreter is the 'evaluator'. The evaluator reads a line of code, evaluates it and returns a result. The line of code must be in the form of an AutoLISP expression.

Quote function

The single quote character (') can be used as a shorthand for the QUOTE function:

`'SAM` *is the same as* `(QUOTE SAM)`
Both return `SAM`
`'(SAM)` *is the same as* `(QUOTE (SAM))`
Both return `(SAM)`

Remember that you cannot use the single quote character directly at the command prompt.

Printing output

Because we have not frequently used the four different print functions you will need to revise the PRIN1, PRINT, PRINC and PROMPT functions.

Test procedure

The following 50 questions will prepare you for the written assessment. Work through every question, checking with your course material in the event of doubt.

Once you have answered the 50 test questions apply to your local college to complete the C&G 4351-005 assessment.

The questions in the written text will be selected from the written competences in your log book. The following questions are similar to those used in the assessment.

In order to pass the City & Guilds written assessment you must correctly answer a minimum of 21 multiple-choice questions in $1^1/_2$ hours from a total of 31.

Good luck!

Written test

1 Name the file used in AutoCAD to automatically load AutoLISP files in the drawing editor:

(a) ACAD.LSP
(b) AUTO.LSP
(c) ACAD.MNU
(d) FILE.LSP

2 Which of the following formats is used when writing AutoLISP files?

(a) BINARY
(b) CDF
(c) ASCII
(d) LISP

3 To avoid leaving a cancelled AutoLISP routine, which will set the OSNAP mode to 'intersection', the following should be included at the start of the program:

(a) (IF *ERROR* (SETVAR "OSMODE" NIL))
(b) (DEFUN *ERROR* (MSG)
     (SETVAR "OSMODE" 0)(PRINC MSG))
(c) (DEFUN *ERROR* (SETVAR "OSMODE" 0))
(d) (WHEN *ERROR* (SETVAR "OSMODE" NIL))

4 Which of the following AutoCAD commands calculate the circumference of a circle with a diameter of 10 units?

(a) PI * 10)
(b) (* !PI 10)
(c) (* PI 10)
(d) * PI 10

5   The AutoLISP evaluator processes AutoLISP programs:

(a) Function by function
(b) Line by line
(c) One programme at a time
(d) Argument by argument

6   Which one of the following correctly defines local symbols?

(a) (DEFUN C:SAM (P1 P2 P3)
(b) (DEFUN C:SAM ()
(c) (DEFUN C:SAM (P1 P2 \ P3)
(d) (DEFUN C:SAM (/ P1 P2 P3)

7   When 'x' = 10 and 'y' = 5, the correct syntax for dividing 10 by 5 is:

(a) (SETQ P1(/ x y))
(b) (SETQ P1(DIV x y))
(c) (SETQ P1(\ X Y))
(d) (SETQ P1(x / y))

8   Which one of the following is *not* an AutoLISP data type?

(a) Integers
(b) Strings
(c) ASCII
(d) Real

9   Which one of the following is *not* an AutoLISP 'real' number?

(a) 59.0
(b) 5.90
(c) 590
(d) .590

10 Which one of the following defines an AutoCAD command?

(a) (DEFUN C:SAM () ...
(b) (DEFUN SAM () ...
(c) (DEFUN:SAM () ...
(d) (DEFUN SAM (COU) ...

11 Which of the following would be the most accurate when calculating the area
of a circle?

(a) (* RAD RAD PI)
(b) (* RAD RAD 3.142)
(c) (/ (* RAD RAD 22) 7)
(d) (* RAD RAD 3.1416)

12   To test the value of a variable 'P1' within an AutoLISP program, which of the following should be entered at the command prompt:

(a) !P1
(b) TYPE P1
(c) QUOTE P1
(d) ?P1

13   Which one of the following would set the variable 'x' = 5?

(a) (LET x =5)
(b) (EQ x 5)
(c) (SETQ x 5)
(d) (SETQ x = 5)

14   Which one of the following is the AutoLISP incremental function?

(a) (1 +)
(b) (1+)
(c) (+ 1)
(d) (1+)

15   Which of the following is an AutoLISP list construction function?

(a) ADD
(b) CONS
(c) CAR
(d) FIX

16   Which of the following is an AutoLISP extraction function?

(a) CADR
(b) CAD
(c) SET
(d) SETQ

17   Which one of the following requires a user input?

(a) GETVAR
(b) GETNEXT
(c) GETENV
(d) GETDIST

18   Which one of the following starts a new line?

(a) PRINC
(b) PRINT
(c) PRINT1
(d) PRIN1

19   Which one of the following is an AutoLISP condition statement?

(a) WHAT
(b) IF
(c) THEN
(d) ELSE

20   Which of the following would convert a string to an integer?

(a) ATOI
(b) ATOF
(c) ITOA
(d) RTOS

21   Which one of the following AutoLISP functions creates a selection set?

(a) SSLENGTH
(b) SSNAME
(c) SSGET
(d) SSMEMB

22   Which one of the following used the correct syntax?

(a) (COMMAND LINE P1 P2)
(b) ("COMMAND" LINE P1 P2)
(c) (COMMAND "LINE" P1 P2)
(d) ("COMMAND" "LINE" P1 P2)

23   Which one of the following AutoLISP functions uses an angle and a distance to determine one point relative to another?

(a) POLAR
(b) RELATIVE
(c) ANGLE
(d) DISTANCE

24   Which of the following AutoLISP functions enable you to set AutoCAD system variables?

(a) SETSYS
(b) SETVAR
(c) SETLT
(d) GETVAR

25   Which of the following would be used to determine the ASCII code value?

(a) ASCII
(b) ASCODE
(c) CHAR
(d) CHR

26   AutoLISP programs must be written as ASCII text files by using:

(a) Word processor (any)
(b) Text editor in document mode
(c) Text editor in non-document mode
(d) Text editor in Windows

27   What data type is obtained when reading data from an external ASCII file?

(a) Real
(b) Integer
(c) String
(d) List

28   What data type is obtained for 'P1' when (SETQ P1 '(2.5 3.6 4.9))?

(a) List
(b) String
(c) Real
(d) Integer

29   The purpose of '\n' in the expression '(GETPOINT "\nPICK THE START POINT")' is to:

(a) Locate the prompt on a new line
(b) Allow a NIL input
(c) Allocate the variable 'N' to the start point
(d) Filter uper-case letters

30   If '(SETQ SAM NIL)' is entered at the command prompt, typing '!SAM' will return which of the following?:

(a) NIL
(b) SAM
(c) T
(d) EMPTY

31   Which of the following will allocate the integer 59 to the variable SAM?

(a) (SET SAM 59)
(b) (SET 'SAM 59)
(c) (SETQ SAM 59)
(d) (SETQ SAM 59.0)

32   Variable 'A' is to be allocated the value of 'B*B' by one of the following:

(a) (SETQ A (B * B))
(b) (SETQ A (SQRT B))
(c) (SETQ A (EXPT B 2))
(d) (SETQ A (SQ B))

33   The following function converts degrees to radians: '((DEFUN DTR (D) (/ (* PID) 180.0)))'. How would this function be used to convert 30 degrees to radians?

(a) (SETQ DTR 30)
(b) (DTR 30)
(c) (DEFUN DTR 30)
(d) (DEGREES (= 30))

34   When 'SAM' is defined as (DEFUN C:SAM () ...) it means that:

(a) Drive 'C' is used to locate the program
(b) Function 'SAM' is a constant
(c) Function becomes an AutoCAD command
(d) 'SAM' is a local variable

35   Variable 'A' is the list '("SAM" 1996)' and 'B' is the list '(1997 "SAM2")'. How can these two variables be combined to give '("SAM" 1996 1997 "SAM2")'?

(a) (COMB A B)
(b) (CONS A B)
(c) (APPEND A B)
(d) (LIST A B)

36   In a routine the variable 'EL' contains the following '((ENTITY NAME: 6910004 >(O. "LINE")(8."SAM")(10 100.0 200.0 0.0)(11 200.0 250.0 10.0)))'. The layer name SAM can be extracted by:

(a) (SETQ A(CDR(ASSOC 8 EL)))
(b) (SETQ A(ASSOC 8 EL))
(c) (SETQ A(CDR 8 EL))
(d) (SETQ A(CDR EL))

37   To enter an input of 'yes' or 'no' with the abbreviation 'Y' or 'N' and presenting a 'null' return, is achieved by:

(a) (INITGET "YES NO")
     (SETQ A (GETKWORD "ENTER YES/NO"))
(b) (INITGET "Yes No")
     (SETQ A (GETKWORD "ENTER YES/NO"))
(c) (INITGET 1 "YES NO")
     (SETQ A (GETKWORD "ENTER YES/NO"))
(d) (INITGET 1 "Yes No")
     (SETQ A (GETKWORD "ENTER YES/NO"))

38   Which of the following will display the screen length 'L'?

(a) (PRINC "LENGTH=")(PROMPT L)
(b) (PROMPT "LENGTH=")(PRINC L)
(c) (PRIN1 "LENGTH=")(PRIN1 L)
(d) (PRINT "LENGTH=")(PRINT L)

39   Which of the following should be used to test whether variables 'V1' and 'V2' are equal to within 0.1 of each other?

(a) (EQ V1 V2 0.1)
(b) (= V1 V2 0.1)
(c) (EQUAL V1 V2 0.1)
(d) (V1 = V2 0.1)

40   If the variable 'A' contains the string 'GOOD' then variable 'B' can be set to 'GOOD LUCK' by which of the following?

(a) (SETQ B (SUBSTR A "LUCK"))
(b) (SETQ B (STRCAT A "LUCK"))
(c) (SETQ B (STRCASE A "LUCK"))
(d) (SETQ B (STRLEN A "LUCK"))

41   The name of the first entity in a selection set 'SS' can be accessed by:

(a) (SSNAME SS 0)
(b) (ENTGET SS 0)
(c) (SSNAME SS 1)
(d) (ENTGET SS 1)

42   Which of the following is the correct coding for drawing a circle having a diameter of 10 units?

(a) (COMMAND "CIRCLE" P1 "5")
(b) (COMMAND "CIRCLE" !P1 "5")
(c) (COMMAND CIRCLE P1 5)
(d) (CIRCLE P1 "5")

43   The function for opening an external file called 'SAM.DAT' which overwrites any existing 'SAM.DAT' file is:

(a) (SETQ FILE(OPEN"SAM.DAT" "o"))
(b) (SETQ FILE(OPEN"SAM.DAT" "r"))
(c) (SETQ FILE(OPEN"SAM.DAT" "w"))
(d) (SETQ FILE(OPEN"SAM.DAT" "a"))

44 A function for obtaining the current drawing name is:

(a) (SETVAR "DWGNAME")
(b) (GETVAR "DWGNAME")
(c) (CMDECHO "DWGNAME")
(d) (GETSTRING "DWGNAME")

45 To determine the length of a line 'P1'–'P2' enter:

(a) (LENGTH P1 P2)
(b) (POLAR P1 P2)
(c) (DISTANCE P1 P2)
(d) (GETLENGTH P1 P2)

46 Which function would you use to create a selection set containing all the circles placed in the 'Foundation' layer?

(a) SSGET
(b) SSNAME
(c) ENTGET
(d) ENTSEL

47 In the 'select-get-search–do' routine, which of the following would be suitable for the 'get' part?

(a) (GET ...)
(b) (ENTGET ...)
(c) (ENTSEL ...)
(d) (ENTLAST ...)

48 Which of the following avoids a 'null' entry when picking points 'P1' and 'P2' with the 'rubber band' effect?

(a) (INITGET1)(SETQP2)(GETPOINT "PICK 2nd POINT"))
(b) (INITGET1)(SETQP2)(GETPOINT P1 "PICK 2nd POINT"))
(c) (SETQ P2 (GETPOINT"PICK 2nd POINT"))(INITGET 1)
(d) (SETQ P2 (GETPOINT P1 "PICK 2nd POINT"))(INITGET 1)

49 To extract the third item from a list use:

(a) (CAR P1)
(b) (CADR P1)
(c) (CADR P1)
(d) (CDR P1)

50   Part of an AutoLISP routine contains '(DEFUN C:SAM (/ P1) ...)'. Which of the following should be entered at the command prompt to run this program after automatic loading via the ACAD.LSP file?

(a) C:SAM
(b) SAM P1
(c) SAM
(d) (SAM)

Index